To my amazing son, Aaron.

When you entered the world, it changed everything for me.

www.amplifypublishing.com

For more information, please contact:
Amplify Publishing, an imprint of Mascot Books
620 Herndon Parkway #320
Herndon, VA 20170
info@amplifypublishing.com

Library of Congress Control Number: 2021910398
CPSIA Code: PRFRE0721A
ISBN-13: 978-1-63755-160-8

Printed in Canada

DAVID E. SATCHELL

EXTRACTING THE
LEADER
FROM WITHIN

AN EXPERIENTIAL LEADERSHIP MODEL OF
INFLUENCING OPTIMAL PERFORMANCE

amplify

CONTENTS

THE FORMULA

THE BACK NINE

THE NINETEENTH HOLE

FOREWORD

KALETH O. WRIGHT

THE FIRST TIME I MET Satch in person was on the golf course. I knew I would like him. He joined a group of my peers following a senior leader conference for a little downtime. He was a genuine person and a real competitor. Little did he know, I had been following his work for quite some time. He had this way of connecting with people through illustrative words, by telling stories that resonated with them and inspired them. His messages were reaching a wider audience than he had thought, and I was thinking, "This guy really gets it." And not only did he understand how to communicate about leadership, but he was also a living, breathing example of what I wanted to see in leaders today.

Satch and I have parallel career paths. Both of us started as dental technicians. Both of us led outside the medical field. Both of us took pulling our influential circles up very seriously.

In 2018, I contacted Satch directly and asked that he join our team at the Pentagon to form a cabal for our senior executive action office. I loved his perspective and energy. He would be perfect for the job. I knew I would be pulling him away early from his dream job as the senior advisor to the executive leader of mobility flying operations, which oversees logistics support in all of Europe and the Middle East. Not only that, but I would be asking him to uproot his family—once again—from Europe to move back to Washington, DC. Of course, there was a bit of resistance, but I was fairly persistent. I remember him saying, "No, I'm good. We are doing good work here."

But I really needed Satch on our team. I asked again. And he responded, "Okay, so when do you need me?"

I replied, "Will August work?" It was June—I knew that would be tough to swallow. With a mild amount of consternation, he agreed— "Got 'em, Coach!"

You see, while Satch was in Europe, I asked him for an urgent and personal favor. I knew if I would just ask him, he would come through. No doubt, he did. That's the type of guy he was. He would say, "Forget about it; I'll take care of it." It was exactly what we needed on the team. I felt comfortable with Satch being in my fairly small circle of trust.

I became the Chief Master Sergeant of the Air Force in 2017—the eighteenth Chief in our history to hold the position since 1967. Looking back, it was one of the greatest career accomplishments I could *ever* conceive—especially since, coming up, I experienced my fair share of failures. Failures that became life lessons. But if it wasn't for Joseph "Pops" Winbush, my mentor, I would not have made it past my first years of service. But once I found my rhythm, serving my brothers and sisters at arms became my passion. Sometimes you just have to be shaken to remind you that your God-given talents are being wasted by mediocrity. Then the light came on. I remember telling a very close friend that I was going to be the Chief Master Sergeant of the Air Force one day. Oddly, she didn't disagree. She saw it in me. It was then when I put my actions in alignment with my purpose—that the idea of achieving these virtually impossible odds became a reality. Many years later, and after a lengthy interview with General Dave Goldfein, it would be announced that I would be elevated to the role. Having been privy to many of the structural designs for developing Airmen, I knew I was going in a different direction. I am much of a renegade anyway, so it didn't take much persuading. I knew if I could just remove a few bureaucratic barriers and traditional hierarchical policies, I could get my colleagues to view leadership from the same lens as me. My advisory team was not convinced. I sat around a table with ten voices of dissent. It was when we committed to our groundbreaking initiatives that our people began to believe in us again. We got to speak about leadership in a holistic way. These kinds of wins opened our minds. Now we are collaborating with industry and refocusing on what leadership truly means. I would do exactly what I was hired to do—be my authentic self and lead from my heart. I was just going to be Kwright. That meant I would spar about concepts of leadership in a collaborative way to ensure our direction was pure. That meant I was going to forge a new selection process that generated leaders based on relevant criteria rather than traditional processes that bred a culture of underdeveloped leaders. If I was happy about anything we got done, it was getting people to think about leadership in a new way that reestablished trust in the hundreds of thousands of Airmen who depended on us.

That is where Satch, one of my few trusted sparring partners, gets it right in *Extracting the Leader from Within*. He exposes the many confrontations about leadership we have glossed over because they are not so black and white. He gets it because leadership is gray and has this amazing emotional element to it—elements of empathy, vulnerability, trust, courage, personality, and character. These elements originate from within and cannot be simply bought or copied. Satch brings these elements to life with vivid illustrations and vignettes, and he shares with you an urgency to deliver on your authenticity.

From the first time I met Satch to the times he sat at the table in my office, next to me in a golf cart, on my back patio, or in a cigar lounge, I knew he was going to stir up a new way of thinking. I trusted him with my own decisions because he had a way of giving me honest feedback about people or processes. Satch had these genuine qualities that were subtly bold. He was grounded and remained true to himself. In *Extracting the Leader from Within,* there is this convergent angle on topics we seldom talk about, and every story he tells breathes in new life and provokes an exigency to reflect. He has a way of making you think about just being you and absolutely not the different iterations of the many people with whom you come in contact. This is where our paths cross. We believe leadership is about being authentic. We believe leadership comes from your personality rather than your authority; from your character, not your title; and from your credibility, not your experience. The true leader is within you. This was my chance to share with you words I always hoped—and in many ways knew—I would have the chance to write about him. And today, as you read this captivating work on true leadership, I encourage you to be more like Satch. Challenge not only the status quo but challenge yourself and your inner thoughts about what leadership really means—you will not regret it!

INTRODUCTION

I REMEMBER THAT FIRST DAY. I showed up to work early. I sat in my car for what felt like two hours. My heart was racing with nervous anxiety. Many years ago my former supervisors guaranteed I would be here in this moment. Today was the day I was going to be put in a position over hundreds of employees. These were the employees who were going to have to trust me and who would hang onto the words I said and hold me accountable. So I would definitely have to follow through. This nervousness had me reflecting and questioning myself: *Am I capable enough for this?* and *Do I belong here?* I wondered if they would like me. I wondered if they would accept me. In a big institution like this, they have seen people like me come and go. So I questioned, *Do I have the ability to motivate and inspire them to new heights?* Because, of course, I came with big dreams and ideas.

My earliest memory starts when I was roughly six years old. I lived with my mother, my older brother, and off and on with six other aunts, uncles, or cousins. I was the youngest in the house. Sometimes it felt like twenty people lived there. Everyone had their space. There were even times when I shared a twin bed with my brother. My mother worked overtime to make sure we had a roof and food. I did not know at the time how much of a struggle it was. We did not have a lot. But I never knew how much we did not have. But I also cannot ever remember being hungry. My best friend, Bo, lived directly across the street. Rain, sleet, or shine, Bo and I would be getting dirty somewhere in an alley, pond, or creek. We were definitely on the hunt for trouble. Bo and his brothers would constantly pressure me to steal a few pieces of penny candy with them at the corner store, and I did. And during the winter, hiding in the cover of bushes, we pelted moving cars with snowballs as they passed. But any other time you were looking for me, I was in this murky, man-made pond in my yard playing with plastic soldier figurines. To this day, I do not know why I do not have Lyme disease right now. That water was so nasty. But during those days, it was absolutely perfect. I have to admit, I got pushed around from time to time. My brother, Tony, and my uncle John thought it was their duty to toughen me up. But I played basketball, football, and wrestled decently, so that helped me keep a healthy circle of friends and some mental and physical toughness. I was a decent student in school, averaging Bs and Cs. Between school and sports, I had a small group of friends. But I tried to avoid trouble. And when it came to partying and hanging out, I was never interested. I have never even had a puff of a cigarette, and my first drink of alcohol came when I was thirty years old. I began going to church on my own, and my circle changed. I received an anonymous scholarship to attend a Christian high school academy just before my senior year. I'm pretty sure it came from someone at the church. But to this day, I don't know who gifted me that opportunity. Other than introducing me to Christ, that community broadened my life's possibilities. Coming from a low-income community tends to obscure and restrict you from those potential opportunities. You end up just circling in survival mode. Getting out of the community, for even just a few hours a week, is what birthed the idea of joining the military. It was never a thought before. And now, after a thirty-year stint, I have visited every corner of the globe and have lived in Germany, California, Las Vegas, the Middle East, Hawaii, South Carolina, New Jersey, back to Germany, then to Washington, DC, and now my final resting place, Tampa, Florida. I remember calling my grandma a few months before her passing to tell her I was promoted to Chief Master Sergeant. She was so proud. It made me teary-eyed. She said, "Baby, we just thought the world was going to tear you apart!" Her reasoning was right. I was pretty nonchalant about things. I spent quite a bit of time by myself nurturing an introverted personality. But deciding to join the United States Air Force was the single biggest life deflection point that could have ever happened to me.

At the beginning of my career, I was simply young, naive, and a follower. I left my small town of Omaha and landed in Kaiserslautern, in what was the former Federal Republic of West Germany. The history books opened up all around me, and I was fascinated. I spent some time traveling and experiencing culture. But now that I was on my own—alone *and afraid*—I really began to learn more about David. That took some time. And since I had a very skewed world perspective as a result of my underresourced midwestern American upbringing, my curiosity was off the charts. But over the next several years, I gained a lot of street knowledge about people. My first indirect supervisor was a young Jewish dentist. He opened my rather ignorant mind to culture, respecting differences, and connections.

I got an associate's degree worth of social structural development from Dr. Carter Kolodny. The next leap came from Lorenzo Bethea while living in Las Vegas, Nevada. I had never met anyone so calm under pressure as this man. No matter how much was thrown at him, he would stop and talk to you and bring a sense of comfort. I cannot say I evolved to his level, but I found myself channeling my inner Lorenzo mental space when things got overwhelming. I have to tell you this story: There was a time I struggled to coexist with a coworker who was a contractor. She knew exactly what button to push to send me to the roof. One of my very best friends, Tom Velarde, and I would commiserate together on how badly we despised her. She was what I called an equal opportunity offender. A number of times Tom and I complained to Lorenzo, and he nodded, smiled, and sent us on our way, encouraging us to work it out. I might add I used a few choice four-letter words when referring to her—I did not like her at all. Long story short, Lorenzo was dating her at the time and subsequently married her. I am still in disbelief how he managed these closed-door sessions about her without pinning us to the wall. My bad, Zo! But throughout my career, I always wanted to pattern myself as a man and leader after him.

I've failed at relationships—one after the other. Looking back, it was my immaturity and insecurity in who I was as a man. Growing up without a father in the home will force you to learn relationship lessons by failure. With no real examples of what strong, healthy relationships look like, it would always be trial by fire. So I whisked through several relationships and slogged through others because I lacked self-awareness and was untrained for intimate connections. Because of that, I received and dealt some hurt in some relationships. I mention this because becoming self-aware is extremely enlightening. Managing relationships and leading people have tremendous parallels in that you use the same skills to lead and inspire as you do to build trust and maintain healthy, intimate, and positive personal relationships.

Moving further in my career, I found myself still as this little fish in a big old pond. When I was honest with myself, I knew I did not have the personality that fit being the one on stage and with a microphone. There were so many great personalities around me who were amazing leaders. When I compared myself to them, I felt I could never measure up. I was not one to rah-rah when it was time to cheer. I was the quiet, informal leader who all my peers came to for perspective. At the time, I had no idea I held this sacred position. But every single day of a promising career, one of my many great inspirations and influences, such as Lorenzo, Tom, Mike Bobbitt, Sandra Box, T. J. O'Connell, Larry Williams, Major General Stephen Oliver Jr., Summer Leifer, Thomas Cooper, Major General Rodney Lewis, Lieutenant General Richard Clark, and Chief Master Sergeant Kaleth Wright, challenged me directly or by example to draw from strengths within me to become the leader our people needed today. And even though I was simply a pawn with a shadow of a crown, I began to realize people looked up to me and trusted me with their careers.

It was not until I obtained my bachelor's in sociology that I could align theory and life experiences together to gain a coherent lesson of people, their primary nurturing influences, social skills, and respect in the form of empathy. It was those lessons that opened my extremely myopic vision of the world into a backbone, a centerpiece, and a foundation of leadership development. I was able to test out my skills as leader and found success. It was then that I discovered the leader was not a created persona or image; it was the strengths that I extracted from within that became influential. My pool of followers began to grow exponentially. And all I wanted to do was share my success and recovery from failures so they, too, could reach their highest potential.

Let me say this: I was a massive failure. I failed at so many things. I failed professionally and personally in epic fashion. But I am thankful my family is so resilient. The Satchells never pitied. And each failure became a lesson I can proudly say I learned and grew from. There are so many situations for which I wish I could turn back the hands of time. But you are not experiencing life until you have dusted yourself off. With failure, there is always a hero. The hero is a close confidant, a parent, or supervisor. I had many. But Karlton Grant was that hero for my biggest career blunder—thank you, Karlton. And so I always wanted to pay it forward and be a hero for someone else. Heroes do not always come wearing a cape. Sometimes they look just like a pawn but with king- or queen-like influence.

So here I go, out from the protective cover of my car, with a brief-case full of lessons learned. I could hear every one of my footsteps, and each of them grinded the scattered gravel into the pavement under my feet. I could eerily hear my increasing heartbeat in my ear. *Crap!* I forgot my satchel. And even though I walked past a few small huddles of people in the parking lot, I could not make out what they were saying. It felt like it was slow motion. One last anxious thought: *Had I prepared myself to be here?* As I swung open the door that had my full name already finely etched in the glass, I wrestled with putting on a smile or a serious face. They all stared back at the door in unison as I opened it. They were waiting on me, and maybe with the same level of nervous energy that I had. I decided on a smile.

Well, here is the moment I always said I wanted a chance at. Here goes nothing...

CHAPTER 1

GRABBING INFLUENCE EARLY

IT IS PROBABLY IMPORTANT TO describe my perspective of influence up front because this entire book is about influencing optimal performance. Influence, in this characterization, is how leaders create environments in which the employees feel motivated and inspired to do the job without the threat of discipline or coercive use of authority. Because when employees are secure and content in their positions, they *want* to do a good job, which makes them more productive. Likewise with leadership, influence is a skillful art and learned behavior to motivate and uniquely inspire others to achieve a desired goal. Establishing influence is done by building healthy relationships, galvanizing trust, relinquishing control, and remaining relevant. Influence is not a one-time transaction—it can be lost. One minute you can have it, then a careless comment, a gross misjudgment, or poor managerial decision can steal back your influence as quick as you secured it. In fact, influence is tremendously fleeting. That is why influence has to be intentional. It is the mindset that you play a role in your team's outcomes. And if you take it personally, as you should, the quality you invest in your influential presence will be the difference. As you get situated and understand your business, remember it is crucial to establish influence early and reflect on it constantly.

Your first time coming into a particular organization and establishing influence was probably not as easy as it had looked. In fact, I bet there was a bit of anxiety that came with your new role. Of course, you want to do a good job and prove yourself. But even with your fortunate position on the upper echelons of the organizational chart, you will have to separate authority and influence. There is no nuance. Your operating baseline is that *authority is not influence.* In fact, 72 percent of the organization's success or failure is attributed to the leader's knowledge, skills, and abilities to motivate and inspire a team. The other 28 percent comes from your team's effort. That is why it is so important to establish your influence early to get them to work *with* you and for you. Some new leaders will enter the organization and establish themselves as the disciplinarian or as the bean counter or even as the overly friendly one. But look at it this way: how the people perceive you is what determines who you are. Trust me, they are measuring you up just as much as you are measuring them. It is a just a matter of time before you get labeled.

What are we actually trying to achieve? As leaders, you are introducing a level of social influence that artfully attempts to change the behavior and attitudes of people to meet the demands of the social environment. The product of social influence is conformity, socialization, peer pressure, obedience, leadership, and persuasion. It is the results of a leader's actions, commands, or requests that cause people to alter their behaviors *and attitudes* toward the objectives based on a perception of what the leader may think or what the leader may do. The social influential effects are not always positive. You can certainly pressure a socially neutral person to behave badly based on the intensity of the influence. In this case, we are trying to achieve social influence by identification. Identification is when people are influenced by someone who is liked and respected, such as a celebrity. From my leadership model, social influence is established by one's unique ability to influence conformity and commitment using personal power's intangibles brought from one's own credibility, courage, collaboration, or character. There is a gravitational and psychological need to conform in environments in which safety and security are targeted and protected, and in which growth and ambition are desired principles. Simply put, social influence's carrier is your personal power. Your people will conform and commit when your personality, character, and credibility connect with them internally.

Grabbing influence can be extremely complicated and time consuming on the front end if you have not acknowledged your strengths and weaknesses. Self-awareness is important here as you begin your employee engagement. Influence will be completely based on the quality of invested time you spend with your people and how they perceive the qualitative investment. Just think if you sat with a worker during a night shift or threw some safety gloves on with a mechanic or wore personal protective equipment with a production worker. It would almost be like an episode of *Undercover Boss*. In just that period of time, you will have shown you were willing to get your hands dirty. Not only that, but you would have learned about all the inner workings of frontline operations. This is the time to be intentional and take notes. When you jot down notes right in front of your people as they voice areas of concern from the perspective of the front line, you will have made an initial deposit of trust—that cannot be underestimated. Trust has a direct link to influence. It shows them that you are listening, that you intend to follow up on it, and that you are taking accountability for the issues. These are transactional imperatives to early influence. I believe there are five you must be thinking about when attempting establish it quickly:

FIVE IMPERATIVES TO ESTABLISHING INFLUENCE EARLY

- Scan the environment and look for unexploded ordnance.
- Establish and communicate your redlines.
- Secure a win.
- Relinquish autonomy smartly.
- Speak the tribe's language.

IMPERATIVE 1

SCAN THE ENVIRONMENT
AND LOOK FOR UNEXPLODED ORDNANCE

If there is not a single important imperative as leader, you must walk the terrain, see the spaces, and view with curiosity. These walks can be very telling and reveal the hidden or unexploded grenades. With grenades, it is just a matter of time before they detonate. The walks are *not* simply what you see. It is also what you hear, smell, and feel. In particular, listen keenly for what is being said and *not being said*—look at what is hung on the walls, desktops, and cubicle spaces. Get a sense of the morale. Your antennae must be up for that. The people who your managers introduce you to or have guide you could indicate how empowered they feel and how much trust they have in their frontline workers.

After your terrain walk of the "front lines," meet with your leaders and middle managers to clear up any real or perceived issues. In my experience, I have found meeting with the entire team and publicly releasing all the issues you have noted and will be correcting shows you were listening, concerned, and now accountable. Setting deadlines and follow-up milestones shows it is important. You will immediately gain supporters—not because you fixed it but because you are doing something about it.

IMPERATIVE 2
ESTABLISH AND COMMUNICATE YOUR REDLINES

Early on, make sure your team knows exactly what your redlines are. Your redlines are the actions or behaviors that are black and white, or in which no tolerance exists. It is my theoretical "point of no return" or line in the sand. If you pass this limit, your safety is not guaranteed. Communicate these early. There is no need for your team to unknowingly trip the line, not realizing these are issues for you. Making it clear sets everyone at ease, especially when they are being made aware of the boundaries. You can take it a step further by posting or putting them in writing. Unclear redlines become annoying gotchas to the team that are completely unnecessary.

Gotchas are the single most frustrating leadership tactic that will guarantee you to lose trust in a matter of moments. Gotchas are those singled-out events, activities, or statements that happen in the open, and you expose them as a failure. Your people will fail in a variety of ways anyway. Do not put them in a position to fail because you have not communicated your redlines. Lying in wait to ensnare your people in policy violations or special instructions is incredibly counterproductive and creates a barrier between you and your team.

IMPERATIVE 3
SECURE A WIN

Following your frontline terrain walk, take advantage of any "softballs" that can be fixed with a stroke of a pen. Softballs are those conditions that you easily apply a stop, start, or change. Your influence will immediately be bolstered. Do not miss this opportunity. If you miss this, you will be relegated to the category of "stupivisors," who are seen as just like all the others. You can guarantee you will hear, "I can't believe this is still a problem! It's right in front of their eyes."

Securing a win is one of the best ways to gain influence. And one of those ways is to identify the thorn that is irritating the team and remove it. Thorns and softballs are not the same. But from the employee perspective, they cannot distinguish the two. Softballs are simple irritants that can be "shooed" away. Thorns are subtle, dug in, and create damage. They are not easily removed, but when they are they provide immediate relief. Be aware that they also leave emotional scars, so make sure you get to the root cause and prevent it from coming back. These wins will build a tremendous amount trust equity.

I have seen examples of leaders securing wins early with intention. Depending on the thorn or softball, that leader could do no wrong going into the future. Just think of the feeling, as an employee, when you remove a ten-plus-year thorn. Regardless, securing a win should always be a victory for the entire organization and team. Simply removing the right thorn can reset the organizational trajectory and result in a huge step forward.

IMPERATIVE 4
RELINQUISH AUTONOMY SMARTLY

The creative freedom associated with the autonomy of your employees tends to be ignored and seen as too risky. Some organizations reluctantly test out this autonomous worker freedom but grab their authority back the minute situations do not go as planned. There is something about relinquishing decision-making that makes leaders and managers antsy. I beg to differ. At any point that you can delegate authority or grant creative freedom, do it! Yes, there's risk involved, but with establishing milestones, you can maintain accountability. When you do, you will garner undeniable trust from your team while you experience a morale increase and innovation boost.

On the surface, the idea of autonomy is a twisted philosophy from the mind of a traditional leader. In those days, the direction of the organization and how each step was carried out came from the deepest halls of the C-suite, not a frontline worker. But the best innovations have never come from executives. We can go as far back as Eli Whitney and the cotton gin. A slave determined a faster and more innovative method to pick cotton—a slave. Innovations come from people who are touching and smelling the materials every day. They know the shortcuts and the gaps. Learning to relinquish autonomy may make you feel uneasy at first. But granting this freedom will be one of the best business decisions you will make.

IMPERATIVE 5

SPEAK THE TRIBE'S LANGUAGE

No one expects you to be the technical expert, although that would be even better. But if you are not, take the effort to learn and understand the language. Lions do not naturally lead zebras. If you could visualize the metaphor, you can probably see the skepticism brewing in that group. You can bet if said lions protected a herd of zebras even the most skeptical herd would get behind its protectors. So, too, would your growing understanding of the team's vernacular yield credibility and an incredulous team's shift from compliance toward commitment to the direction of its leader. Understanding the language of the team has a value-added impact on the relationship going forward. The longer you delay learning their language, any influence you may have built will likewise diminish.

KEEPING IT REAL LEADERSHIP

I am sure you have heard someone say, "I am just keeping it real." In fact, I am sure you have heard it time and time again. When I have heard it used, it is followed by a statement that usually does not align with how things are actually playing out. It is a statement that says I have been or am going to be a renegade. But when you think about what it is associated with, it is typically a marginal idea, decision, thought, or action. I bet there is someone standing within earshot that is *not* fully supportive of the comment or decision they are about to take. Why is that? If keeping it real is socially acceptable, why does it always seem to be a disclaimer?

On the flip side, keeping it real means speaking with candor. It could suggest you have stepped out with professional courage. I don't disagree that keeping it real commands a space in our place of work, because we need candor. We need the conversations that say, "This just isn't good quality work," or "You could have put out a better effort," or "This is unacceptable," or "You need to work on your professional appearance." It also may communicate back to leadership that you are not very supportive, or you are doing a poor job managing.

DOES KEEPING IT REAL SIMPLY EXCUSE PENDING BEHAVIOR?

From a leadership perspective, the problem with keeping it real is that it often outcasts someone else by its connotation. But with candor, it addresses the issue and does not *feel* personal. Now more than ever we need to elevate candor. Because when candor is left out of conversations, it sets up our leaders, teams, or colleagues for failure. It leaves out an important detail that could even necessitate scrapping an entire project because we were completely off course. Over time, candor has been left out because of its seemingly provocative nature. It exposes a person or process for what it is. We struggle with candor because in our nature we would rather water it down because we are not comfortable with pointing things out directly to its culprit.

So how can we keep it real but not lose our teammates? Here are the steps to making "keeping it real" work effectively: 1) establish a relationship; 2) there are no further steps. When you have a relationship, you can speak with candor, and the other party does not take offense. They know you do not mean harm. In the workplace, candor is essential to getting it right the first time. In fact, a leader who facilitates an environment in which the workers can keep it real can ultimately increase productivity and potentially operate with limitless efficiency. But candor without relationships almost always *seems* personal. And speaking with candor to your boss without having a healthy understanding of their perspective can have some unintended negative consequences.

I get it. It may not be natural for you to speak truth to power or be frank with your peers or coworkers. But your organization and each of its team members are depending on it. Fostering an environment that each can keep it real will always start with trust and healthy relationships. It is your responsibility to model the behavior you want to see in your team. Show them it is acceptable, and there are no reprisals that stem from it. Then you will see keeping it real across the organization, where teammates are helping one another through constructive critiques. If leaders are in the business of increasing optimal performance, they will set these conditions. Ultimately, colleagues who speak with candor but without *intentionally* inducing hurt feelings will see performance metrics skyrocket and morale increase.

As you develop your leadership talent, you will learn that candor and fostering open communication is a key quality and an imperative for stakeholders, investors, and even the customer. But it is not a license for an unbridled tongue-lashing intended to set the record straight. Because that is reckless and will get you fired. But the distinction between keeping it real and candor is that your input will ultimately be constructive or shine a light on a blind spot. Let's not forget the bottom line: increased shareholder value and mission success are at stake. Listen up when you hear someone preface a statement with "I'm just going to keep it real with you." They just *might* have valuable input that helps you or the team.

> ### "EMPLOYEES DO NOT QUIT THEIR JOBS; THEY QUIT THEIR BOSSES."
> —GALLUP POLL OF ONE MILLION US WORKERS, 2009

There is certainly a correlation here when only 28 percent of the organization's success is accounted for by the team's effort. That leaves 72 percent being attributed to its leader and their ability to set the conditions for success. Your ability to establish influence early is crucial, especially when shareholders are deeply invested or even when lives are on the line. Here is your opportunity to steer the outcomes of your organization by the manner in which you lead it. Having influence is not predatory. It is simply exercising your personal powers of personality, character, and credibility to motivate a team to achieve the shared goals of the organization. Influence is not only about employee relations. It is about removing the barriers that act as obstacles to team performance. Your supportive contributions make you a willing participant and not just a bystander. Your abilities to remove or thwart those obstacles are motivational acts to individual performance. Your people get excited when you enhance the physical and social conditions of their environment. When you do, they reciprocate by working that much harder, triggering increased optimal performance.

As you read through the rest of the book, reflect on how your influence changes the workplace. As the motivational vehicle to their performance, your ability to see the environment and its barriers with clarity will afford you opportunities to build trust. You will find influence comes in a variety of forms. You will see it in your communication. You will see influence in your social skills and in your ability to regulate your emotional behavior. You will also see influence simply in your self-awareness. As you understand who you are, you can motivate and inspire the team by exposing those natural strengths within you, and not replicas of your leadership heroes. Of course, this will make you a little vulnerable, but that is the exciting part about it. It is your vulnerability that shows your courage, your credibility, your character, and your collaborative nature, which outwardly validates the trust. And trust is the foundation to *your* influential leadership efforts and *their* entire commitment.

CHAPTER 2

TRUST ON TRIAL:
WHEN THE BOSS IS TOO IMPULSIVE

THE MOMENT THEY HAVE REALIZED they have really screwed up at work, you have a chance to respond. You have seen screwups before. All of a sudden, they stop in their tracks, their mouths drop wide open, and they look to their right and left to see if anyone spotted them. It is remarkably similar to when you trip over that tricky crack in the cement sidewalk—we have all been there. But the realization that they have really made a terrible error will test what they are made of. And even more importantly, how will you, the boss, react? We all know that particular boss who will "flip his lid." He's been known to go off the rails and on the attack by pointing, raising his voice, getting personal, or berating a vulnerable employee just seconds after they have unwrapped the wrongdoing. And because the team knows this about him, they often use the tactic of avoidance or refuse to report bad news to him.

Let's talk about this. Anger is a simple human emotion and no different from the others. Emotions like happiness, grief, nervousness, or disgust all nestle within the same emotional sphere as anger. You may have heard the "fight, flight, or freeze" response when addressing reactions to increased emotional stimulations. Anger is one that traffics in this similar basic survival mode. And believe it or not, the behavior that coincides with anger is learned and inadvertently nurtured in the developmental years. Coming also from the sympathetic nervous system, anger readies you to fight. Fight in the form of combating behaviors, injustices, or even laws prepares you emotionally to stand up against it—not just physical combat. Because anger erupts from the same mental space as other reactions, accessing the appropriate level of emotions can at times be uncontrollable. This happens over time, when imbalanced hormones have disastrous effects on the mental space, specifically the brain's neurons, and weakens its ability to control exhibiting anger.

If you are honest with yourself, you can admit if you are *that boss* with the short fuse. You know, the one who gets fired up seconds after someone misses the mark, sees red on a PowerPoint slide, no-shows, or does a task in their own unique way. This self-control thing can and will drive an organization to its knees. But the number-one effect that stems from a lack of self-control is loss of trust. Yep, it is the trigger to putting trust on trial. And if you do not get ahold of your wily impulses or emotional outbursts, no one will ever, *ever* come to you—for anything.

Leadership begins with trust. It is the foundation to your relevance. Without it, you will only have superficial relationships and meaningless influence with your workers. The most misunderstood realization about trust is that the leader does *not* get to determine its presence. It is completely follower discerned. When the team corroborates the existence of trust, they will expose trust's three freedoms: vulnerability, fidelity, and audacity. All three freedoms advance the organization.

- Vulnerability: open to critique and personal attack.
- Fidelity: a sense of being one with the whole.
- Audacity: showing the ability to take bold risks; having courage.

In a well-run, high-performing organization, employees who are open to these freedoms will raise productivity and have a willingness to fail forward because there is no threat to being *vulnerable*. They have the freedom to be *audacious* and to take pride in ownership of their craft, finding creative methods to improve organizational performance because their sense of *fidelity* with the team is rock solid. The products of these freedoms are commitment, engagement, and open communication among the team and *directly* with the leader. But don't understate fidelity. It is that sense of belonging that all employees want and need—the sense of being in a safe space to learn, grow, and contribute. Of the three freedoms, vulnerability's strength has its sensitivities because of its perception of threats. When vulnerability is intentionally exposed, left out in the open, and employed, its greatness shows no limits.

Being audacious is the far-right limit of empowerment. It is innovation's palpable pulse. Having the audacity to think outside the box is a freedom few dare to explore. But when leaders react poorly to botched attempts of failing forward, it weakens those bold, risky behaviors that have a potential to catapult an organization forward. When a team is taking risks and trying something new, there must be safe space to fail. And failure must be accepted in an organization. Effective leaders must be of the mindset that failure to innovate is taking a step back while all other innovative organizations step forward. When leaders respond negatively to audacious attempts or even react poorly to inadequate results, innovation ceases and so, too, does the momentum of the team.

The correlation of vulnerability to performance is widely overlooked, but it is essential to the current work environment. It is not a trait we fully invest in, but we count on our frontline workers to be open to communicating innovative improvements to organizational processes. Vulnerability is innovation's personality in that it exposes thought processes and the exploration of unchartered territory even when *sometimes* there is a lack of confidence in the change progression. Daring to be vulnerable is a test. Any attack on one's vulnerability will force them back into their shells *and sometimes* never to come out from their protected cover again. Trust goes on trial when you are not able to regulate your response to this sensitive process, which is a critical step to influencing optimal performance.

Conversely, lack of trust is the absence of these freedoms in your organization. That means your people are guarded and looking out for themselves. They will accomplish only the bare minimum, which flattens productivity. Under these conditions, innovative initiatives will cease. When trust is lost, workers will cover up errors. They will avoid management, and communication will be intermittent. Breaks in trust become scars on relationships because they violate important expectations. All these conditions just because of the boss's apparent lack of self-control.

BRENDA

I met Brenda early in my career. She was the senior manager of an office of seventy-five or so workers. Brenda was from Texas and always reminded you of the customs and norms of Texans. As you know, Texans are overly proud and line up just below Puerto Ricans for the proudest countrymen title. Brenda was no different. Brenda was brought up with an old-school method of "do as I say." She did not prefer any back and forth. Brenda was a single parent of a boy in college at the time. She was also responsible for caring for her ailing mother, who lived in the home with her. Brenda made all the decisions about how things were going to be. After being assigned to the organization, I had been warned of Brenda's fiery personality. It did not take long. I got to observe it with my own eyes. She leans in, raises her voice, sometimes points, and talks fast. And oftentimes some would leave Brenda's office as if they had been in tears. There was another side of Brenda. She would smile and tell you stories. She would enjoy calling me into her office and telling me a story or two of her many experiences. She loved reminiscing. I think she was fond of me, but I was not sure. I think I reminded her of her son. One year for Christmas, the office bought Brenda two figurines of dogs—one of a rottweiler and one of a poodle. We told her to place the appropriate dog on the desk conspicuously so we knew what kind of mood she was in. She got a kick out of that and actually used them. I remember most of the time the rottweiler was sitting out. Nevertheless, when Brenda got fired up about a phone call she received, confirmed or unconfirmed results, or the performance of one of my peers, you could hear Brenda walking through the halls, hearing each of her steps from her heels angrily tapping the stone floors. The faster her feet were moving, you could tell how big of an issue it was. And no matter the issue, big or small, it got the same elevated emotional response from Brenda. Initially, it was shocking, then it began to be annoying. You would hear people say, "Why does she have to be like that?"

And others would say, "I will never, ever come to her for anything."

When things got tough, the team would agree to send me to her office to talk her off the ledge. But even I did not know what to expect. All I can say, Brenda did not mean any harm. She wanted things done the way she wanted them, and with no back talk. Brenda had a lot going on in her life, so she would always be on edge. The problem was, very few knew how to take her. And because she reacted this way notoriously, they were not interested in getting to know her. The complication in all of this was that she had an unbelievable team of motivated professionals. But Brenda's predictably unpredictable responses kept the team from getting better. They were not motivated to do anything for her. Too many feared her. Unfortunately, the team just did not trust her, because they did not know how she would react. Only if Brenda had some control of her reactions—other than the Tasmanian devil—she would be the ideal manager for this group.

Self-control, or self-regulation, is *a strength* and a key component of emotional intelligence (EQ). Influential leaders *must* maintain a high level of EQ and be aware of this behavior in themselves and others. I will address EQ throughout the book. It is a *power* that many struggle to tame. Having the ability to control your emotions, including the expressions of them, is a peek inside of how you handle difficult situations. And depending on the intensity of the circumstance, your emotional behavior will tend to parallel the mercury meter's uprising. The strength is having control of a wily and untamed behavioral response. Like training a pet to behave in certain manner, it takes time to challenge those emotions when they are put to the test. From a more cerebral perspective, you must identify those triggers that set you off so you recognize beforehand and avoid them as you grab control of it. Simply put, activating events or anything that sets you off drive a behavior. But when you slow it down, you have complete control of it by your thought process. Just think of the time when you were cut off at high speed on the interstate. Like many of us, you may have sped up and given the careless driver the "you're number one sign." You may have mean mugged them or had a few choice words. All these reactions came with thought. And with each of them, you could have chosen against them. Here is the proof: If you noticed they were a big, burly man or a senior citizen, you would have tamed your behavior accordingly. It is a matter of seconds, but you have the strength to choose your behavior.

The American Board of Psychology defines *impulsivity* as behaving without forethought. That would mean the behavior is not without thought, but it is behaving without negotiating the consequences. The tricky quandary of impulsivity is when the behavior works out; then it encourages this continued spontaneous behavior. And one step further, the behavior can be misconstrued as bold, courageous, or daring when in fact it was likely reckless and unpredictable. You can bet that some leaders use the pretense of impulsivity for a short-term win—meaning, a shock-and-awe effect directed toward their subordinates to reclaim their authority. Although this act may create the desired effect, it is short lived and so off-putting that it gets ignored in impending episodes. This is when the buildup of trust gets wholly bankrupted. The effects of uninhibited conduct and the strength of trust are completely tied.

As you can see, impulsivity comes with tremendous consequences. No matter how difficult the circumstances may be, the boss must extinguish the fuse and realize any outbursts will have long-term effects. More importantly, you should be concerned with bystanders who have now learned "there ain't no way I'm coming to him when something goes down." There is danger in these public outbursts. You can easily multiply the loss of trust by simply not being aware of your surroundings. The outcomes of impulsive behavior will show no bounds. You can ultimately lose your *entire* team. When their confidence is shaken, they will begin to take orders from informal leaders *and not you*, and they may or may not share your strategic perspective or just may even contradict it.

THE DILEMMA OF A WORKPLACE BLUNDER

According to her orientation training records, Joannie had signed off on it all. In fact, her trainer and the learning manager have initialed it. But over a period of time, Joannie's performance had been degrading, and you saw it happening in real time. Joannie was a sweet young lady. She was someone all could call a good friend. She was pleasant to be around at work or hang out with on the weekends, where she would often be out and about with her son. But at work she tended to sit at her seat and do just about anything to never get up from it. Every time you passed by, you saw Joannie appearing to be working hard but cutting multiple corners. Eventually, something would go wrong, as Murphy's law would surely prove true at some point. Oh, look! Today is our day.

"Damn it, Joannie!"

Encountering a big workplace blunder from a colleague can get complex. As a leader, you have to resist being impulsive. I am sure you will realize upon arrival to fatal error ground zero there were targets of opportunity that were missed to reorient Joannie's actions somewhere to the left of "bang." But now you are confronted with a vehicle or equipment mishap, an irrevocable process error, a key customer complaint, or injury on the job—it is all overwhelming and never timely. And after you clean up the workplace crime scene, you will have to address what went wrong—your theoretical fork in the road. Of course, the majority of inputs you will receive will point toward, "Fire her!" Although that is certainly an option, is that the right thing? It was a mistake, after all.

I believe the response to these kinds of critical errors that impact organizations fall in only two categories: training or discipline. Look no further. There is almost a certainty that people problems can be resolved by exploring these two paths. And if it were me, I would always evaluate training first. Not just Joannie's training but also the training program itself. We can be talking about errors that provoke a dip in shareholder value, create a massive future reinvestment of a resource, or cause a loss of a key customer or account. Those are *whoppers*. But we are also talking about errors that are recoverable but create setbacks, either financially, by timelines, or output—the big *annoyances*. Either way, they have to be handled with the same level of care:

Was Joannie trained?

Did Joannie show proficiency?

Was Joannie familiar with the equipment and precautions?

Was the quality of the training comprehensive?

If there is a no to any of these queries, I would take the nuclear option off the table. Errors occur every day, but when training is substandard the potential for errors escalates exponentially. Let's stop and take a breath. Hold back all the career tributes (a *Hunger Games* reference) and examine your own organizational training regimen along with the member's individual training. You just may find you have a system problem, which you own, rather than a people problem.

Terminating an employee in haste or on the basis of fuzzy evidence can cause more problems in the long run than the ones you think you are solving. Let's talk about that. Firing or even relocating an employee has remarkable effects, obviously on the individual but also the team. And depending on how valued the teammate was, the effects are magnified. Unbeknownst to you, rumors begin to stir, and the facts surrounding the loss of a teammate unravel. Not only that, but coworkers also evaluate their own mortality within the organization. Now you have a morale and a trust issue because of the perceived threat of getting fired due to a mistake. Bottom line: firing an employee cannot be impulsive.

After a sound examination of your training program, you will be forced to evaluate the discipline that led to the blunder.

Did Joannie follow the checklist, guidance, or your instructions?

Was Joannie careless in her performance of the tasks?

Did Joannie willfully cover up the mistake?

Handling disciplinary issues can get emotional. It is one of the tougher issues to deal with as a young leader. To be frank, it gets fumbled quite often. So keep it simple. It is all about communication and conversation—that is, not only transmitting information (communication) but also exchanging information (conversation). Your emotional intelligence quotient will be tested, especially with a combative employee. Because that will be the time when you show your self-awareness, self-control, empathy, motivation, and social skills—all the components of emotional intelligence and all of them at the same time.

On-the-job blunders can get really messy. You have to commit to the two paths to address the issues with purposeful precision. Do not let the training path look like discipline or let discipline look like training. Follow the path until it cancels itself out. But if it is indeed disciplinary, make sure it is clear and policy supports it. If you set a precedent that mistakes get you fired, your team's productivity will plateau, individuals will become overly careful, and your trust will be doubted. You can guarantee the word will be out with whichever decision you make. Even if the meeting takes place behind closed doors, word will soon reach the entire team. So, while you have an opportunity to carefully explore the issues, take a look at both training *and then* at discipline. For Joannie, we trained her again to guarantee there were absolutely no inadequacies in her training or the program. Going forward, it was easy to determine that discipline was her demise. Unfortunately, we had to let Joannie go.

> **YOU'LL KNOW YOU HAVE A TRUST ISSUE WHEN YOU LEARN OF PROBLEMS THROUGH THE GRAPEVINE.**

You could easily lose your cool with Joannie early on. And Brenda just could not uncross the wires. These are experiential examples of how impulsivity and decisions can set the temperature of the organizational environment or change the course of peoples' lives. You know the drill—count to ten! Abracadabra! Talk to yourself or get beyond the surface of things. But whatever technique you use, I implore you to acknowledge and communicate what trips the wire and always have someone *you trust* to hold you accountable—just own it. There is guaranteed to be times when your employees really screw up. Getting fired up is one way to address it, but it usually will be destructive and will end with your apology. In your haste, you could make the determination to terminate someone's employment when there could possibly be opportunities to retrain or reorient an employee. Because of this, the team perceives that you knee jerked the situation, and now they have concerns about their own employment mortality. If you had navigated the decision tree, you may have still ended up with a similar outcome. But it is not the outcome that is in question; it is the impulsive and hasty behavior or decision-making that was careless with someone's career. Being frustrated is a natural human response, but the manner in which you verbally and nonverbally react can shift the organizational climate—a climate in which you own.

Just remember: trust is front and center, and it is on trial.

CHAPTER 3

THE SAFE SPACE OF LEADING BY AUTHORITY

SOMEWHERE DOWN THE LINE YOU will have been selected to a
managerial role with a big or small organization. I wonder if you had
thought about what approach to leadership you would take. Have
you ever thought about it? I hope you have. After all, you will have
just secured the coveted new title. And just like that, you will have
the responsibility to advance the organization to meet its objectives.
Would you take more of a democratic style in which collaboration
would reign? Or would you take more of a laissez-faire style in which
you would be more hands off? I know there are some who would
begin with more of a transactional style in which rewards and discipline would be the incentive to behavior and outcomes. As you
can see, there are several types of approaches. Depending on your
personality, you may choose the coaching style in which you spend
a significant amount of time developing the skills of your people. If

you do, you would push some to take on challenging new roles to stretch them and perform at higher levels. You could even start with an autocratic style. If you do, you would closely manage processes and the strict compliance to policies. You would be the decision maker for all things and empower very few, if any, to assure procedures are tightly controlled. I know many say they would not, but situationally this style is necessary. Of course, most managers are not gifted a perfect organizational climate with skyrocketing productivity; therefore, you would have some work to do. And one of the most important initial decisions you would have to make is your approach to engaging your employees. I wonder if you ever thought about it. This is not one of those questions you leave to the back of your mind, where you allow your unconscious thoughts to make decisions. You have to know that your approach cannot be haphazard. It *really* needs to more intentional.

The absolute safest approach is to simply act upon your authority. You know, your name tag, your seniority, or whatever the guidance manual states. Acting on authority means you can issue orders, mandate procedures, and punish disobedience. You will not ever be compelled to engage with your team. And even safer, you will not be bothered with winning the confidence or trust of your workers. In the corporate world, your authority is often your geographic position on the organizational chart. In the military, of course, it's the amount of adorned brass or stripes, or it may be even your assignment to scarcely reserved parking spots. You can easily recognize who the authority is, and most of the time they will just tell you. Here is the thing: People simply do not respond well to authority. And if you think about it, the only real reactions that are elicited from your position of strength are compliance, fear, intimidation, or indifference. The problem is that it is absolutely no way to influence optimal performance. Acting on authority will only yield minimal compliance and nothing more. Leading by authority has a shadow side. The shadow side is also called an unconscious side. Through an effort of purposeful self-awareness, one becomes aware of their shadow. The shadow has a naturally negative connotation; however, it is not intended to be.

SHADOW SIDE OF AUTHORITY

- layers of bureaucracy
- presence of politics
- disengagement
- unpredictable turnover
- increased absences

The jury is still out on authority's definition. Social scientists have added modifiers because authority has distinctions in a variety of empirical settings. So people just decide on their own what it means and how they act upon it. What is it about authority that leaders in the workplace begin with it to drive action? I would bet those put in these positions resort to acting on authority because it limits the retort and back-and-forth communication of their commands. Authority affords you the luxury of not having to connect. In its purest form, it is the preference of one-way communication and enforcement of obstinate directives. When a leader has not fully developed their innate strengths to drive commitment, using authority as a buttress bears some comfort in guaranteeing compliance. You cannot mistake that authority is a concept of power. Power represents one's ability to motivate by a variety of means to achieve an end. With power, you can be recognized as the person in charge, the one to gain approval from, or the one to *not* get sideways with. But because of that, you will find that these managers who traffic in authority will plant layers of management between them and their people to ward off varying degrees of engagement. Even more so, because of their underdeveloped social skills, they avoid their people on the front lines because of their lack of confidence to connect. And finally, acting on authority can be a learned behavior that stems from strict parenting, coaching, or teaching. Because of this, it winds up being part of one's own character. When it is seen as something that is effective, it is adopted as a foolhardy leadership technique—it is exactly that. So how one defines it, chooses to leverage it, or determines what setting to exercise it is often measured against how confident one is in their leadership skills. At some point, you will have to get *beyond* the boundaries of authority's protective cover to profoundly influence optimal performance.

ARVIN

You will not forget the day you meet Arvin. Purposefully or not, you are guaranteed to remember that moment. Arvin makes sure when he introduces himself that you know he is in charge. He also made sure you understood that decisions flowed through him. Every time I went to his office, I had this physiological change. My heart beat a few more times per minute. My attitude changed. My shoulders dropped. I took several deep breaths. Even though I did not fear him, I hated going to his office because he made mountains out of molehills, and I would rarely be in the mood for it. He sapped my energy before I even got there. Arvin had the typical modus operandi. He dressed perfectly, used foul language, and he never looked at you eye to eye unless, of course, he was trying to intimidate you. Arvin always got the last word. And somewhere in the conversation, regardless of the subject matter, he would remind you again that he was in charge. I am not quite sure why he did that, because everyone knew that. In the break room, everyone would talk about how they rerouted their paths to meetings and tasks to avoid Arvin that day. I am convinced Arvin made us do ridiculous and menial jobs just to prove he was the decision maker. The problem, if we did not need anything else, was when interpersonal issues rose Arvin would badly mishandle them. He was the type who would use a sledgehammer to tap in a nail. I have a feeling he just could not find the empathy switch when he needed it. And if he predicted that a situation called for being empathetic, he would call Tim. He knew Tim could handle it and get to the bottom of it. This always made me believe he knew his shortcomings because he had Tim on the hotline when situations called for it. Tim was the team's filter, negotiator, and interpreter for Arvin. If you needed something to get approved by Arvin, you asked Tim because Arvin liked Tim and trusted him for some reason. Oddly, Arvin knew people would go through these charades to get things done. But the strangest thing about Arvin was when you had an opportunity to sit with him on the patio or in some nonthreatening environment, he was such a great guy for the time. And that was it. If you got that opportunity, you became utterly confused about the experience you were having and the person who was before you. You would laugh at his edgy jokes and enjoy the back-and-forth discussions about football and sitcoms. He knew the details and all the stats. You walked away thinking, *Where was this same guy during work hours?*

There is a lot to unpack when it comes to an authoritarian personality type. There are sixty shades of an authoritarian, and it manifests differently in social settings. In a nutshell, the personality type looks at things in black and white. They have an allegiance to acknowledging authority and do not mind showing aggression for those who oppose their trains of thought. Authoritative personalities, like Arvin, look at people with distain and a wholly negative view, even if they do not recognize it in themselves. They look at leadership as a position of strength that should not be second-guessed. Arvin certainly took this position, deliberately or not, because it guarded anyone from opposing him. Those who do will be embarrassingly put down to prevent others from mounting a resistance. Creativity is looked at as an effort to overthrow their authority because they are clear on how they want a particular task or action accomplished. Finally, authoritarian personality types display a veneer of toughness or anger, so their authority is never in question. Not all authoritative types exhibit every shade of the personality. And that is when it gets complex, because out of the blue a nice gesture appears, and you are taken aback by it. You see, it is a self-esteem issue that has to be addressed. You just have to have courage to address it. If or when you do, you will find they experience some degree of security in their role.

Acting *beyond* your authority is not so safe. In fact, it is a defenseless space to be in. It is the space in which you lead with personality, character, competence, courage, or credibility. I would consider it leading by your personal powers. It is a fragile space because personal power generates human emotional responses. And emotions are fleeting and sometimes irrational, making it increasingly unsafe. Because it is *so fleeting*, you will need to support personal power with other sources of power, like information power, connection power, or reward power, to stabilize its consistency. Until you have established strong relationships, one misstatement, a bias, or skepticism can easily slip in and challenge your new and forming connections. The trickiest part about personal power is when you will have to issue unpopular orders or, even more so, punish disobedience, which are all safe acts of traditional authority. But you will be amazed how accepting your people will be of your candor and discipline when you come from a place of authenticity. And when your personal powers are fully engaged, you can ignite motivation even from a disciplinary session. You will see retention increase, innovation becomes present, and commitments to the team fuse.

BENEFITS OF PERSONAL POWER

- increased loyalty
- collaboration
- trusting environment
- improved communication

To be fair, there will come a time when your personal power alone will not prove to be enough. This is not the time to abandon it. Hold steady. It is a position you should never depart from. This is when you must introduce other mechanisms to influence compliance as you nudge them toward commitment. Disciplinary write-ups, a transfer out of a job, or removal of perks, all are attention getters as you remain grounded as an influential leader acting on personal power. In my experience, I have even terminated a worker's employment because I was not able to achieve basic compliance. On the way to the door, he said, "I would not want to be fired by anyone else. Thank you for treating me fairly."

This goes to show that even though you may brilliantly execute personal power, your people have a vote and may *still* not be motivated.

I get it. "Because I said so" ends the constant questions and maybe even affords you a preemptive strike to the queries, "Why do we have to do this or that?" In the end, the workers will get it done, even begrudgingly. They will *comply* just to avoid any expected reprisal from their defiance. Like I said, it is a safe approach to management. Make no mistake, this is *not* leadership. But when you use language like, "I chose you particularly because of your talent," or "Based on the intent, I'd like for you to use your expertise to come up with a solution for," employees will tend take on a new level of commitment to the organization. Yeah, it is unsafe because you do not know *exactly* what product you will receive or response you will get in return. But you have enriched your employee engagement and opened the lines of communication. That cannot be measured.

> **"A SHIP IN THE HARBOR IS SAFE, BUT THAT'S NOT WHAT SHIPS WERE BUILT FOR."**
> —JOHN A. SHEDD, 1928

Here is your bottom line: If you are striving to influence optimal performance, you have to lead *beyond* your position or position description that deems you as the one in charge. And it is critical that you convince yourself it is acceptable to tread in the unsafe waters of personal power. Just know the riskiness of vulnerability and the outward expressions of your own unique qualities, bundled up as your management style, will be the avant-garde of influential leadership. Vulnerability and trust are tightly aligned. And all leadership models sit on a foundation of trust—a little or a lot. If your intent is to build commitment, it is the only way. Acting on authority *will not* do it. Personal power is the long game, with a consistent investment in connections, communication, and collaboration, all built on a firm foundation of trust. Cleanly put, vulnerability and trust are personal power's one-two punch.

Acting on authority alone will only breed compliance. And compliance is the act of doing exactly what you are told. It is working by the letter of the law or according to a set of rules. In these environments, innovation and empowerment are not given oxygen. Think about it: Is your organization just putting in the hours and giving you nothing more? Are you *not* hearing "Hey, I have an idea"? Are employees not coming to you with issues and just making it work? Are you hearing "That's not my job"? These are all the sounds of a compliance-driven organization. And if you are hearing these sounds, have you thought about what your leadership approach is doing to provoke these kinds of responses or feelings? There are a number of leadership approaches and management styles to choose from. Did you determine which is the best fit for your organization? And if you are tuning into these responses, these are all indications you may be treading in the safe space of authority, and your leadership style needs to elevate to the next level.

Jump on in—the water is fine! I even have floaties, if you need them.

CHAPTER 4

LEAD LIKE MIKE

MICHAEL JORDAN IS ARGUABLY THE best player to ever play the game of basketball. Along with his six world championships in the 1990s and career-lead scoring campaigns—every baller wanted to "be like Mike." Mike was raised in Brooklyn, New York, in his first five years before his family moved to Wilmington, North Carolina. He was an amazing multisport athlete in basketball, baseball, and football. Mike was cut from the varsity basketball team as a sopho-more, but because of his success in junior varsity and his four-inch growth spurt, he was selected to play on the varsity team in his junior year. As a high school senior, he was selected to the McDonald's All-American team and subsequently recruited to the University of North Carolina—Chapel Hill by the late hall of fame coach Dean Smith, turning down several scholarships at competing universities. Mike astonished basketball fans throughout his college years. He went on to be drafted by the National Basketball Association's Chicago Bulls. It is with the Bulls that he became the greatest. And during his time, he cheated hall of fame–caliber players from winning world championships. You could even put an asterisk on the Jordan years to justify their HOF selections. There have been many who have been compared to his skill, but the argument never changes—he is the greatest of all time (GOAT). And certainly, if *you* want to be the GOAT, you will have to pattern yourself after the greatest to do it. Although this is about basketball and a phenomenal basketball player, why can't the principles apply to leadership?

We all come to the table with our own talents—talents that certainly do not measure up to Mike's, but talents nonetheless. The qualities you bring to your leadership capacity are not always perfect. But like Mike, you practice them until they name them after you, like his amazing dunks or his fade-away jump shot. And if you know anything about MJ's story, you will know he tried and failed and tried and failed again. Leadership is exactly like this. It is this unique process of human creativity based on your imperfect strengths. It is an art. And an art is a specific thing acquired through practice; therefore it is rare, if at all, to come naturally. What aspects of your leadership art are you practicing?

Building on your talents is critical as a leader. Talents like effective communication, team building, motivation, or relationship building—these are some of the strengths you must be working on to be an MVP leader and manager. Mike's talent as an athlete opened the door to being a basketball player. But it was his unrelenting practice of the game that made him great. In similar fashion, the practice of a variety of aspects of leadership will make you an influential leader. For instance, not all of us are great communicators, one of the most underdeveloped talents among managers. I have discovered leaders tend to also have underdeveloped listening skills, an inconsistent delivery of rewards, a lack of empathy, and poor social skills, all but guaranteeing they will never be an MVP without putting them to practice. Have you thought of what aspects of your leadership art you need perfecting? I hope you are at least thinking about it. But if there were talents I believe influential leaders should be highly skilled in, they would be in critical listening and verbal communication. I will talk more about communication in chapter 13, "Verbal Communication: A Lesson from the Natives," but let's pull that thread on listening.

Listening is a tough nut to crack because *you* have something to say, and it *must* be said. But listening is *not* hearing words. That is tantamount to a dialogue with Charlie Brown's teacher. Listening is hearing the words, processing the context, considering the nonverbals, and making sense of it all. The science behind listening suggests people do more reading and less listening during their physical development. And because of this, less people have trained their cognitive minds to remain attentive and engaged as they are being addressed. There is more texting, more social media, and more swiping left than actual time spent in conventional conversations. People tend to process their responses too early in the sender's message. And if you are to hear the words, process context, consider nonverbals, and ensure it makes sense, there is no way this can be done midsentence. To bridge the gap, senders and receivers form wild assumptions and often-inaccurate conclusions to cover what was unheard. Leaders just have to be comfortable with a pause between the back and forth. Initially, it will be incredibly awkward. But when you train your mind to critically listen *to it all*, you will find you are a more effective listener and have more success at being responsive to your people.

"WHAT GOT YOU HERE WON'T TAKE YOU THERE."
—MARSHALL GOLDSMITH, 2016

But why like Mike? In the mid- to late 1980s, Mike could not even *sniff* a championship nor was he good at leading his team. Throughout his career, Mike missed a number of game-winning shots—shots that really mattered. But the quintessential Mike got up and promised to be back better than ever. Ironically, no one ever remembers those shots. But as a leader, you have to recognize your talents and apply them judiciously. Mike finally owned his failures, worked to build a better team, and *only then* did he and the Chicago Bulls become arguably the best ever. There is a popular quote that says, "What got you here won't take you there." The talent you exhibit today will not be what you need as you advance. Do not be so arrogant to believe because you sit in a position of leadership, even at a high level, that it affirms you do not have flaws in your presentation. So evaluate those good and beneficial qualities that you rely on. Determine the ones that need to be enhanced. Read, learn, and study about those strengths and their effectual application.

MIKE

One day I was raising hell with three of my peers about them not helping with some of the dirty work everyone else had been doing. These three held the perspective that dirty work was for everyone else, and not them. So, as I am standing just inside the door giving them the business, I had this odd intuition that someone was standing behind me. It was Mike. Mike was this big, tall, pale, and bald-headed white guy. He had this odd smile you could not read. It could easily be inviting or a preparatory expression before something very bad was about to happen. I looked back at Mike. But since I did not know who he was, I returned my attention back to the three big-timers and finished my thought. I looked back once again and Mike was still standing there with the same expression. I noticed his name tag this time and put two and two together and realized he was our new boss. I apologized for ignoring him. He said, "I loved the way you handled that. It got a me emotional." Mike was a former policeman. Visually, you could easily tell. But as you got to know him, he was an amazing leader who got everyone involved. If you showed a propensity to lead, he would throw opportunities your way. He was a hard worker and got his hands dirty. The one thing about Mike: he understood the essence of empowerment. He never needed the glory. He let his team shine. Mike had also the mentality that "everyone would pull their own weight." If you did not, he would let you know. That is when the LAPD in him came out. He had this way of admonishing you. His cadence had no breaks in it. He would clearly communicate his dissatisfaction. His facial expression never changed so you were not distracted by nonverbals. There was one thing about Mike, it would always be about the team. Mike rose up the promotion ladder too. And as he did, he would share his knowledge and put effort in making sure the top workers were recognized and rewarded. He spent no time on those who did not. And held each of us accountable to making sure we dealt with "dead weight," as he called. it. Later on, as our relationship developed, I would learn that Mike was a father from a previous marriage. He and his wife had lived separately for quite some time because of work, but he never appeared distracted by it. I would bet his work-life balance was poorly adjusted. Mike had the same personal challenges many of us all suffered from, but somehow he was able to compartmentalize those struggles and gave us the best of him. Mike was an extreme motorcyclist. He would travel to all fifty states in a ten-day period. One time he traveled to the Canadian and to the Mexican borders in a twenty-four-hour stint—crazy. I only mention this because Mike had an outlet. This much time on the open road I would assume he had a lot of time to negotiate situations in his head and find clarity. But no matter what he was dealing with, you would never know it. And whenever I got stuck, personally or professionally, Mike was clutch when it came to advice. I credit him for my "clean sword" approach to discipline. Just because you were being reprimanded, it did not have to get loud, emotional, and out of control, but you absolutely knew you were being cut. Mike would go down as one of the top influences on my career and life.

The challenge of leadership is to always be at the top of your game. There is a tremendous amount of pressure to being all things to everyone at all times. It is an unreasonable ask. After all, you are human and must accept that as fact. You are guaranteed to have "life happen" from time to time, and *sometimes* you will report to work with an empty tank—then what? There will be one thing you absolutely must arrive to work with: a high tolerance for people. When that is too much to ask, it will be time to cash in one of those personal days and call a time-out. There is no shame in that. Mike Jordan had a metaphorical scenario during the "flu game," in which Mike scored thirty-eight points in game five against the Utah Jazz in 1997. During the game, he vomited and even had to be carried to his seat. In that condition, he had one thing in mind: win game five. My point is that not every single day will you be in perfect physical and mental condition. But when you suit up and enter in the arena, it takes this minimum aspect to have in mind to *still* put on an MVP performance—tolerance for people. Your people expect you to show up every day with your emotionally intelligent qualities at the ready:

- self-awareness
- self-control
- empathy
- motivation skills
- social skills

To be self-aware means that you have a realistic understanding of your social status and what you are presenting in real time. Self-awareness is a strong quality that some, when they are not honest about it, trick themselves into believing who they are and what they represent. When you are honest about it, you have willingly accepted the imperfect individual that you are and recognize those strengths and weaknesses that you walk around with every day. In essence, it is your ability to recognize and understand your moods, emotions, motivations, and their effects on others.

To have self-control means you understand your emotions and know how to regulate them when activated by a number of unplanned and uncontrollable scenarios you will face throughout a day. It is the regulating of an insatiable tendency to react to matters usually that you hold as important. The actual act of self-control happens at a point between an activating event and its corresponding behavior. High EQ leaders have the ability to control or redirect their disruptive impulses and moods. They have the propensity to suspend judgment and think before they act.

To respond with empathy means to connect and respond on an emotional level that is equal to the other. Although empathy is an emotional connection, it has a cerebral aspect. It takes a mental adjustment and change of nonverbals, especially your tone, to plug into the wavelength that suddenly is directed at you. An individual exhibiting a high degree of empathy is able to understand the emotional makeup of other people and treat them according to their emotional reactions.

To have motivational skills means you can uniquely inspire individuals to take another step toward their goal. Since your people are motivated differently, a high EQ leader has the ability to motivate and influence in varieties of methods. Talented leaders can motivate beyond the carrot or the stick.

To have social skills means you have proficiency in managing relationships and building networks. I refer to it as an ability to persuade people who do not look like you. When you have a high degree of social skill, you can enter any group of people—old, young, gender, race, ethnicity, hip-hop fans, and quilters. Social skill is a fundamental strength that is underdeveloped. In fact, in my thirty years of leading, never once had this necessary skill been intimated as an expectation. Having social skills allow you to be inclusive. This is critical when you need to make every employee part of the team.

I bet you are a skillful leader in your own right. You have gotten to your position because you have influenced optimal performance for individuals, your team, or your entire organization. Like many of us, we rely heavily on certain innate and learned strengths and purposefully subdued the ones that are not fully developed. Some lean solely on their intellect. Some hide behind their charisma. And some manipulate by masking their lesser strengths by accentuating their connection power. It is time to stop concealing them. I would venture to say that there is an employee *just wishing* you were better at certain characteristics of your art. In Mike's early years, he was rapidly transforming into the best ever, but he could not magically produce enough wins for the team on his own. He certainly had the strength of athleticism and ability to score in bunches. But it was his underdevelopment as a team player that kept the Bulls from getting to the next level. And just like Mike, it will be something other than your primary strength that holds you back as a leader. Hiding your weaknesses will only hamstring you from your greatness. All your skills need work, and you have to be willing to practice them. Be like Mike. Get in the gym until you have fully developed them. You may even find you have a skill they will name after you.

CHAPTER 5

DEVELOPING EMERGING LEADERS

JUST THINK IF YOUR ORGANIZATION's leadership development program was deliberate, or at a minimum, just existed. I say just existed because it is one of the big misses in businesses nationwide. I cannot imagine there being bigger managerial responsibility, because one of your many enduring obligations as a leader or business manager *should* be to recruit and retain talent. This should be high on your list, right? Quite honestly, organizations on a national scale do not do a very good job with this critical function. The key reasons are typically time, risk, and perceived return on investment. In my estimation, leaders have been chosen arbitrarily or by some antiquated promotion system that focuses on managerial tasks and very little on employee relations techniques. By the looks of the high-profile ethics failures across the nation, there is certainly room for improvement. But why have business managers risked this crucial process? Maybe because it takes real effort to be future invested when the demand of now is right up on you. Maybe it is because leaders today have been so bogged down with what is immediately in front of them that they neglect opportunities to potential future leaders. The real risk is they buy into single points of failure. That is when one person owns the corporate knowledge of the place. It gets even riskier when an individual is the only one who can bridge gaps in how the organization is run. To avoid all of this, leaders must prioritize incorporating an emerging leader program that buys down the risk, especially to the bottom line.

There are some sincere advantages to building an *internal* developmental program because they are already tested against the cultural fitness of the organization. Developing internally as opposed to hiring externally gives you greater assurances that the collective values align with the organizations. Studies show that 60 percent of employees who navigate through the internal developmental pipeline tend to perform significantly better than external hires. Confidence is raised, and morale is boosted because employees feel their efforts are valued. Like I have always said, morale equals productivity. When your people see themselves growing with organization, trust and confidence is built, and motivation increases, all but guaranteeing a more productive individual or team. Why then would leaders not invest in building a robust program to identify, develop, and promote internally? If it were up to me, here is how I would structure *my* emerging leader development program to protect the future of the organization:

1. Search for and recognize leader potential and begin building a bench. Of the myriad attributes, these are *my* eight minimum essential qualities:

- demonstrate integrity
- history of productivity
- act as team player
- influential among peers
- reliability as a communicator
- sees the big picture
- takes initiative
- inquisitive learner

2. (Experience) Assign them to shadow a high-level or critical position.
3. (Training) Share the strategy, mission, vision, lines of effort, and important performance indicators and financial key metrics.
4. (Education) Enroll emerging leader to advanced professional or technical courses. Offer them access to digital classrooms, if available.
5. (Training and Experience) Personally mentor or assign a mentor to closely observe their actions, time management, communication, and decisions. I would key in on the following:

- How they link daily tasks to the strategic goals and objectives.
- Their familiarity with policy.
- How they report data and problems to management or the C-suite.
- How they communicate with their team.
- How they solve problems and deal with complexity, mistakes, or failure.

As you can see, I recognize development in three parts: education, experience, and training. Education consists of formal classroom or virtual training that imparts and tests their theoretical, doctrinal, or philosophical comprehension of the specialized area. Experience is the sum of time of being assigned to and involved in the specialized area, specifically as a change agent, supervisor, or in quality control. Experience is *not* time. An individual who has been *present* is not necessarily experienced. Training is the rigorous exercise in the area while being able to touch, see, smell, and hear the operation and the materials used in the specialized area. When you prioritize these micro-opportunities for education, experience, and training, you increase confidence and more importantly eliminate single points of failure.

As a leader, you have a responsibility to constantly probe for gaps in talent while looking for leadership potential. You cannot wait for a vacancy to begin developing employees to fill these gaps. The talent is right in front of you—it just needs to be explored. There is nothing wrong with giving your people opportunities in specific areas in your system. You never know when you will call upon them. If any of your top performers voice interest in key areas or cross-functional training, consider them as part of your list of emerging talent. You will find some are potential leaders and some are untapped talent. Equally, just because an individual voices interest does not mean they should proceed to the track. You should always evaluate them against your minimum essential qualities. If you want to preserve your experienced talent and raise the level in the organization, start with an emerging development program.

> "ONLY 7 PERCENT OF ORGANIZATIONS BELIEVE THEIR LEADERSHIP DEVELOPMENT PROGRAMS ARE BEST IN CLASS, ACCORDING TO HARVARD BUSINESS PUBLISHING STATE OF LEADERSHIP DEVELOPMENT SURVEY."
> —TILDSLEY, 2016

I keep hearing managers say, "I don't have time for these kinds of programs." But all it takes is one equal employment opportunity event, mismanagement, or mistreatment of employees, a dip in shareholder value, or a sudden vacancy in a key position to instantly "find time" to realize the return you get by investing in an emerging leader program. I guarantee you will find time to then scan the organization for a replacement who does not bring on risk. I bet you will find time to identify a replacement with more rigor. When you do, you will advise them on ethics responsibilities, show them how you would like them to engage with the people, and you will build in feedback milestones to ensure they remain within the guardrails. Because after a leadership blunder, your focus and time will be on finding the right replacement. You get it? It is the same amount of time you would invest in an emerging leader program, or what I call building a bench. You just have to decide if you want to build it before or after the leadership gaffe. So let's be clear: You do not have to be at the highest level of leadership to build a program. You should be constantly thinking about your gaps and your single points of failure. Those gaps should be your starting points until you have a more deliberate and robust program. Front line, middle managers, and senior managers should all be thinking and putting in time to analyze their bench performance.

SHEILA

If your company's computers suffered what would be an irrevocable loss due to some kind of system failure, of course, you would call Sheila, who works in the thirty-five-person IT section. Sheila is übertalented and knows absolutely everything about IT. The company management calls Sheila *directly* for the toughest jobs. Sheila analyzes the IT issues, and even if it would take over twenty-four hours to get the company back online, Sheila will have saved the day! As a business manager, of course, you, too, would have your eye on Sheila. She has the talent that any organization would want. She is your go-to resource.

I forgot to tell you: Sheila can sometimes be a pain in the ass. She can be resistant to change. And even though she can fix anything, you usually have to search her out. If you are looking for her, she normally can be found at the smoke pit. Sheila tends to be in the middle of any and all workplace drama. Most business managers would be afraid to lose her talent, so they do not ask too much of her, even though the company is growing at a rapid pace. Management was hoping Sheila would develop a network monitoring system to detect when the systems were degrading as a preventative measure. But Sheila is hesitant. Since none of us speak the IT language like she does, we count on her to do those kinds of things.

And finally, since Robert, our IT section manager, is retiring, Sheila is the likely candidate to take over for him. Rob is the kind of guy who makes things sound so easy. At the manager meetings, when issues are being called out, Rob is taking a bounty of notes. By the time it gets around the table for him to speak, he has figured it all out. Rob knows the exact technician to put on every job. But he also knows when to say no. When he does, the management team is confident the ask is beyond the scope of the organization and will concede the issue. But the best part about Rob is he can motivate his team. He has the right kind of personality for a busy support function that needs lots of attention. They all seem so willing to help and check back with you after they have installed a new innovation or fix. It was one of the requests from Rob to his team, and they were fully committed to it. So it is simple, right? Sheila has the most talent. Take your strongest performer and make them your leader—voila!

Wrong! But that is how it is done in leading organizations facing the need to select their next leaders. They conflate mastery with leadership. Mastery is expertise, proficiency, and certification. Leadership, in stark contrast, is the art of influencing optimal performance in an individual or team. Sheila is your clear example of mastery. And right now she is not your example of leadership.

In this scenario, Sheila did not exhibit my eight minimum essential qualities. As a result, from the onset, Sheila should not be selected as an emerging *leader*. Let us acknowledge that every individual is not cut out for leadership or performing a leadership role. There is definitely no shame in that. But let's not throw the baby out with the bathwater. And even though Sheila does not exhibit the qualities we seek in emerging leadership talent, we owe her a clear discussion on her future with the company. But first we are obligated to give her feedback on our observations and a discovery of what she is willing to improve before we move on or shift in a different direction. Some people just need to be tapped with the wand of self-awareness.

So, before you move on, have this conversation:

- "I have been observing your performance ..."
- "Are you aware your behavior led to ..."
- "These are the qualities I am looking for ..."
- "I'd rather put you in more of a skilled track, where your

talents can flourish. What do you think about ..."
- "Let's set up a monthly feedback session ..."

This goes to show that developing emerging leaders might just cause developing emerging *talent*. Talent is precious and needs to be elevated, including skilled technicians. Telling an employee they are not cut out for leadership can get emotional. The idea of management passing on them, even when they have little interest, makes them feel some kind of way. On the other hand, you may even discover they find some relief in the satisfaction that they do not have to assume a leadership role. It is the kind of candid conversation missing in our organizational culture. In this case, Sheila loves the mastery aspect of her job that she can come to work, troubleshoot, and solve IT problems. For her, it is personally fulfilling to bring computers and networks back to life. As leaders, we have to respect that and set her on a path that leads to her personal development as well as our organizational growth.

The function of leaders is not simply to build more leaders. It is more involved than that. If you reduce it to purely this purpose, you will miss out on the talent right under your nose. Focusing on leadership alone creates an up-or-out system that overlooks talent, including some late bloomers. Depending on your level of leadership, you want all concentrations of leaders thinking about building their benches within their sphere of influence with their available talent. Midlevel managers should be filling gaps and resolving single points of failure by developing the talent in the indirect roles that a single individual has routinely been occupying and maintains the corporate knowledge. God forbid you lose that person.

What does it mean to build a bench? If you understand any team sport, a general manager, coach, or owner who is heavily invested in the team's outcomes would never hinge it all on single high performers. Of course, they invest deeply in second- and third-string reserves as much as their key players. Even the best teams that are performing at the top of their class, conference, or leagues are just an injury away from being the worst in that same grouping. As a result, the backups train with the starters. Not only that, but they are expected to know the game plan to the same degree as its potential predecessor and must be ready to step in at a moment's notice. To take this a step further, they are expected to know the plays, the language, the audibles, and the contingency plans. And even though they get fewer reps in the day-to-day flow, the expectation is high. The expectation is even higher when your reserve could substitute in the highest leadership positions.

I get it: identifying leaders takes time. Many will focus on the concentrations of hot talent. I cannot emphasize this enough: talent *does not* equal leadership. And while you separate the two, you should never compromise your own minimum essential qualities that you require for a leader on your team. As you select them, your more senior-level managers should be focused on revealing the connected dots to these up-and-coming high potentials. This means connecting the day-to-day tasks, decisions, and outcomes to the overall strategy and financial performance of the organization. It means opening their eyes to the big picture. It means showing them how their work aligns with the up and down stream contributors. And finally, it means understanding its risks, its competitors, and its customers. If you do not, the learning curve becomes too steep, and the spin up time becomes overwhelming. Understanding how the pieces come together in the operation should not be their first exposure to the process when it is time to take the position. This must be more deliberate. The time, risk, and return on investment are obvious here.

As a leader, it is up to you to take on the purposeful responsibility to build an effective bench and grow a thriving, well-led organization, the results of which will be your return on investment.

Do not wait. Start building your bench today.

CHAPTER 6

DEVELOPING AND CULTIVATING MASTERY

In the previous chapter, I introduced a full-throated distinction between leadership and mastery. Also, in my blog post "Leaders and Masters Sometimes Appear as Doppelgangers," I made a case that mastery is often disguised as leadership. But what I hoped you would learn is that leadership requires some unique qualities that are not *always* evident in subject-matter experts and mastery. Of course, this is not an absolute. Mastery is the strength of an individual's expertise and level of responsibility in a given field. Throughout an organization, there will be levels of expertise, with very few considered experts and a proportional number of developing experts. These individuals are *not* your organization's leaders but have potential to be. But what we have seen is that organizations select their leaders from this group of subject-matter experts and heavy producers instead of selecting them from a set of criteria that values emotional intelligence, courage, collaboration, and character. It is a cultural conundrum. Don't get me wrong: classic masters *could* exhibit a wide range of qualities—that of leaders *and* that of masters. But often they do not. Today's organizations have created up-or-out promotion and retention systems that focus solely on building leaders and have taken for granted expertise until they absolutely find themselves in a pinch. But to remedy that, it is essential to elevate the conditions of mastery because it is vital to the organization's bottom line—market competitiveness, mission effectiveness, or shareholder value.

So what is it about leadership that it is distinguished from masters? In the previous chapter, chapter 5, "Developing Emerging Leaders," I listed *my* minimum essential qualities to be a leader in *my* domain. Those were:

- demonstrate integrity
- history of productivity
- act as a team player
- influential among peers
- takes initiative
- reliability as a communicator
- sees the big picture
- inquisitive learner

But what about mastery? How do we treat our subject-matter experts who do not exhibit the leadership qualities our organizations need? Discounting the value of expertise can be deeply damaging. But the answer is quite simple: hold them to the minimum standards of the organization, reward their goal achievements, challenge them, and have open communication about their performance. There will be experts who want absolutely nothing to do with performing in a leadership role and will threaten to resign if they are forced. Some leaders are even troubled by this logic. I would caution against forcing a person into a leadership position, even if you see the potential.

You simply have a one-on-one discussion about what you expect of them going forward, and you both will find inroads to increase performance and continue on their developmental path until they are ready. I would reinforce performance targets and set stretch goals to match their individual talent level. But here is a crucial misjudgment that you will have to confront. That misjudgment is the failure to invite your experts to a seat at the table. They are your critical cogs to leadership's blind spots. Giving experts a voice at the decision table increases commitment to the team because they feel valued in their position as an expert. Their technical awareness can and will prevent bright idea disasters and increase innovation opportunities. When leaders inspire and motivate their experts, you will find the quality of performance increases, and metric milestones are exceeded day over day when they typically would remain at or near the average. I would also offer that expert commitment can equally raise the performance thresholds that leadership sometimes cannot.

Experienced workers who are proficient in their craft need a very different kind of leadership style. They need the freedom of two-way conversations and feedback. You should relinquish your stronghold on empowerment and give your experienced workers creative freedom while maintaining accountability for the tasks so they can remain productive as possible. On the other hand, you should not shy away from teaching "old dog new tricks"; experienced workers need to be shown new techniques like all other employees. And just like awarding freedom of two-way conversation, give *their* learning style the benefit of doubt. Your masters may be so far advanced in some areas that you would need to be guardians of their time, just as your own, by forgoing lengthy presentations of unnecessary theoretical background.

Leaders often have a "you're dead to me" attitude with those who are not trending up or even toward the leadership track. They are often treated as expendable. This is a colossal mistake. We absolutely must retain this talent, so you will need to develop, motivate, and advance your masters. And not only that but develop a career path that masters can see themselves growing with the business. The cost of onboarding is too great to undervalue what subject-matter expertise brings to the table. You will have to humble yourself and acknowledge what they can and do offer. So, if you want a well-run organization, you have to tap into the creative genius that your workers impart. Pilots have to feel comfortable with their copilots holding the wheel, and sometimes your expert co-pilots will have better ideas and understanding than your experience and position brings. There is strength and leadership maturity in relinquishing autonomy smartly.

The military, other than the United States Air Force, offers a warrant officer program in which they select from subject-matter experts to put in a talent "track" to elevate experience and proficiency. Their primary task in their role is to serve as a technical expert, provide valuable skills, guidance, and expertise to commanders and organizations in their particular field. In this case, the military has raised expertise and rewarded them with a parallel rank structure. In the corporate world, there is not a similar effort. Often organizations are on strict budgets, so offering raises are not always prudent. But incorporating an experts' reward system to increase motivation will also drive productivity. Designing promotion opportunities in technical fields and investing in their expertise shows the organization values their proficiency.

LINK

The very first time I met Jeff (we call him Link), I was rushing into a staff meeting for the first time on my very first day on the team. By the time I got in the conference room, Link was speaking at eight decibels higher than I had normally experienced. Nearing the door, I heard several four-letter words that again are not commonly shared in this room. Surely, the boss had not arrived, and Link must have been chumming it up with a peer. But no—Link was sitting at the end of the big table, knee-to-knee with the boss. "This is the worst fucking plan for a trip I have ever seen!"

I was like, whoa. The boss took it very cool and responded, "Link, then what do think we should have done?"

Okay, pause. Never in my career had I seen or heard a junior-ranked employee speak to a senior officer in that manner. It did not stop there. As I scanned the room, there were several other senior officers in the room listening attentively and apparently the object of Link's objections. "You, for one, really screwed this shit up when you did the survey!" as Link pointed out the culprit.

"We'll talk more after this meeting, Link," the boss replied.

Link was an amazing talent. And he knew the business better than anyone on the team. People relied on his expertise to get better as an organization and more effective at delivering results. Link won the respect of his peers and his bosses. Because of that, it granted him an amazing amount of latitude when it came to determining how to proceed forward on operational tasks. The one thing Link was not good at was leading people. Don't get me wrong: I would go out on any mission with Link because it was guaranteed to be a success because he knew exactly what to do and when to do it. Somewhere during the trip, Link would have pissed off half the crew. But all that turmoil was lost when we returned home to account for a successful mission. In fact, there was nothing but smiles and laughs. Link would admit, "I'm not great with that leadership stuff, but I know my job!"

Every year, when it was time to compete for promotion, Link would go into the testing room, Christmas tree the answer sheet, and come back to the office ready to work. He was, once again, bypassing an opportunity for a leadership position. But looking back, it was probably for the best. Link had talent and exceptional expertise in the operations world. But motivating and inspiring was not his cup of tea. The one thing that was a semblance of reward for Link was his ceded control of operational tasks. The boss gave him carte blanche authority. No doubt, being empowered was his reward, and it incentivized him to keep performing at a high level. Link was one of a kind. And just as stunned as I was with my first encounter with him, I knew not every junior-ranking operator could get this kind of treatment.

First, I do not suggest that anyone should *ever* be given the freedom to speak to their boss in this manner. This was an extreme exception and permissive in a culture of another time. There are some unique organizations in which this freedom is sanctioned, but that should be the exception, not the norm. In this case, Link was afforded a seat at the table and a voice. Second, it is a rare occurrence to have such an expert that exhibits so little leadership talent that they would be bypassed for promotion over and over. But beyond that, how do we grow and develop a person like Link to continue to be the cutting edge of the effort? It is obvious his kind of talent is needed. He exhibits the strengths we want to see in mastery. Forcing Link into a leadership role could be counterproductive. And at some point, you will have to reorient him to a mastery track.

I must reemphasize that there has to be an incentive to keeping masters motivated. And as much effort as one puts into building an emerging leaders' bench, one must use that parallel energy to develop and retain their talent. That means, once more, promote them to their relative value, invest in their technical development, create a performance goal reward program, put them in positions where their skillsets influence higher productivity, and again, most importantly, give them a voice. If you value and treat masters like they *are* essential to the organization rather than an expendable commodity, you will achieve optimal performance without breeding a climate of haves and have-nots. If you do not, you will notice your talent will begin looking for greener pastures.

STRENGTHS MASTERY BRING TO AN ORGANIZATION:

- exceptional performance
- history of productivity
- attention to detail
- skilled technician
- ability to connect the dots
- determined
- problem-solver
- subject-matter expertise

LEADERS AND MASTERS SOMETIMES APPEAR AS DOPPELGANGERS

Here I go again! Again talking about leadership and the nuances to being influential. Quite honestly, if you Google "leadership," you can find fifty-eleven-thousand—my technical term for a lot—studies, commentaries, and distinctions on the art. And with all these studies, you would think there is nothing else that could be said on it. And because there are so many studies, you are led to believe that this is really important stuff. And furthermore, because of the demand and appetite for learning more, you would have to determine there are just not that many people who are good examples of it. Why is that?

It is just leadership, right? So I will just throw it out there.

Warning—seminal statement: Not *everybody* is cut out to be a leader.

For some, that will not sit well with them. And for some others, based on their experience, their heads are nodding emphatically. So I will say it again for those in the back, not *everyone* is cut out to be a leader. What I mean is, not everyone should be placed in a position of leadership just because they desire to be in that role. I realize that leadership has a sexiness to it that people believe they have made it when they secure the position description. Don't discount the animal nature of humans. People naturally want to be pack leaders. When they are not, they experience grumpiness for a time until they find their rightful position among the pack. Leaders have a set of unique and innate qualities. And not everyone freely demonstrates those characteristics. Some people are cut out to be exceptional workers, technicians, scientists, artists, doctors—you get what I mean. Some may be die-casted to be disciplined managers. Wait, let us be clear: managers and leaders are not the same thing. And being a manager is not subordinate to being a leader. Let us also be clear, being the best at your job, your art, your talent, or your skill, does not also qualify you as a leader. The unique qualities of leaders come naturally for some. For others, leadership comes along with some trial, error, and lessons learned—it did for me.

There is an exhausted list out there on what qualities are composed of a leader. I have my own. Mine are not unique, and quite honestly, they fall within the scope of the many leading studies on leadership.

- character
- courage

- competence
- collaborative

So, if it is just as simple as these four qualities, why can't just about anyone be good at it? I am sure the vast majority of you believe you exhibit these qualities. But here is the secret sauce: emotional intelligence (EQ) is the multiplier and personal power (PP) is the carrier of those qualities—see my formula. For emotional intelligence, a person has to exhibit a high level of self-awareness, self-control, motivational skill, empathy, and social skills. For personal power, a person is obliged to present an array of optimism, confidence, vulnerability, and communication skill.

There it is! Emotional intelligence and personal power are the critical elements that separate influential leaders from the rest. And this is what makes some not cut out to be effective leaders. Again, I know this does not sit well for some of you, because our culture and natural order has demanded us all to be leaders. But I would argue that the demand is misguided. There is room at the inn for all the many qualities, skills, and talents, and we need to reward each of them, just like we hold Albert Einstein, Isaac Newton, and Steve Jobs in high esteem. These same experts are not known for their emotional intelligence and personal power—they would readily admit.

ROLES OF MASTERS

- technical experts
- training managers
- safety managers
- problem solvers
- internal controls

Today we have failed to elevate mastery as par to leadership. We have put leadership on a pedestal and made an unfair distinction between those doing great work and those who are influencing and empowering them. So it is time to elevate mastery, the doppelganger that is sometimes disguised as leadership. It is time to put a face to the masters of your industry, your organization, or your team. They may not be cut out to be a leader but your organization cannot survive without them. Because we conflated masters and leaders, people are having a tremendous time distinguishing the two. They are our generation's doppelgangers. And even if I define and disassociate the two, people are compelled to make them synonymous—they are not. So the study on leadership continues. And I will have more to say.

Reading the above list mastery's strengths, I have no doubt some of these terms aligned with your concept of a leader. You are not wrong. I would argue the nuances between the two are in the areas of communication, being a team player, and being influential. They are the cornerstones for leadership and *desirable* for masters. An absolutely winning formula is an individual that exhibits both. But often the pair are seen as unicorns. For one, communication is the ability for your people to hear and understand your perspective—not only that but you also understand theirs. When the conversation is complete, each of you will feel enriched by it. This is a critical quality in leadership and beneficial in mastery. To elevate mastery, leaders sometimes need to take a step back. Like a point guard in basketball, one passes to the open teammate or lobs a pass for the other to score. So, too, is your role as a leader. Stepping back and allowing your experts to bask in their apparent glory shows your maturity and relevance. Being influential suggests that your presence increases performance, changes attitudes, and raises commitment. If leaders do not recognize and elevate these strengths in mastery as essential to the organization, you will sustain an inner tube's slow leak and will not be aware until you are stranded with a flat.

So let's elevate mastery and watch your organization outperform.

CHAPTER 7

THE X FACTOR: CULTURAL COMPETENCE

IN MY EXPERIENCE, THERE HAS been this one elusive skill that has
become the elephant in the room. It is a skill that is rarely brought to
the surface and seldom discussed in open conversation or training.
And frankly, it is taken for granted. People just believe that others,
and certainly their leaders, have mastered this skill by the time they
have been put in this position. To be honest, somehow this skill has
slipped into and was folded in under annual sensitivity or equal
opportunity training, when it really is a study of social structure.
At the risk of elevating this to a scientific study, it is critical that
leaders understand the diverse patterns of social norms and social
systems. These are the unwritten rules that are deemed acceptable
but are approached differently in a unique society. Shaking hands,
man space in a public bathroom, or speaking with eye contact are
those norms expected across a wide swath of American society. But

a basic understanding of social structure in leadership development has been treated largely theoretically. In a global working environment or mobile societies, you must be able to consider and appreciate these patterns that exist between individuals but still make up a coherent whole. Our societal complexities and diverse beliefs are astonishingly different under one roof or in a virtual meeting room, and too many leaders have a monolithic approach to people because they are ignorant of social systems or deny its existence. When this is dismissed, I see it as leadership negligence. Why aren't these lessons being introduced formally? In the twenty-first century, why aren't we having these conversations openly? Because the skill of cultural competence is so elusive that leaders who *do* show proficiency bear the X factor of cultural competence in an area that very few have integrated in their leadership development.

Cultural competence is the ability to understand, communicate with, and effectively interact with people across cultures. Cultural competence encompasses being aware of one's own worldview, developing positive attitudes toward cultural differences, and gaining knowledge of different cultural practices and worldviews. To bridge the gap, first, one would have to acknowledge your own worldview. Then you would also have to maintain some degree of appreciation of other views. When your view collides with your appreciations and you dismiss other views, you will fall very low on the competence meter. Those who are open to cultural differences and appreciate the differences from others have a high level of competence. But not only that, those who integrate that understanding into their leadership development carry a maximum level of competence. To understand cultural competence, it is important to grasp the full meaning of the word culture first. According to scientist and author, Steven Chamberlain, in *Recognizing and Responding to Cultural Differences in the*

Education of Culturally and Linguistically Diverse Learners (2005), culture represents "the values, norms, and traditions that affect how individuals of a particular group perceive, think, interact, behave, and make judgments about *their* world." That would mean there are multiple views of your shared space and neither of them are wrong. As a leader, what are you doing to see your space from different angles?

ANTOINE

Let me introduce you to Antoine. Antoine is from South Carolina. He was raised by his single mother in a remarkably poor neighborhood. Around his kitchen table, Antoine, his grandma, his mother, and brother talk about what happened over the week. It is rare they get this time together because his mom has two jobs and comes home late, even after Antoine has gone to bed. So Antoine and his brother unload all the details at the table. After they are finished, Antoine is reminded of a few things that have invariably been drilled in his head: don't trust them just because they wear a uniform; I don't care how bad you are hurt—you better not call the ambulance; be tough—don't cry; and nobody will ever do something good for you just for free. These themes somehow were mentioned at every talk around the table, every single time.

If you think about it, Antoine would definitely be one of your many workers. In fact, there are hundreds of Antoines standing around you—I guarantee it. Antoine would be a really good technician but a bit socially awkward. He would pride himself on being a lady's man. He would do what you would *feel* are some questionable things from time to time. And he would get a bit rigid when being held accountable. You would notice his face and what you *believe* would be this "I don't care" attitude in his body language. Often, when confronted, he would say, "Why didn't you say that to Alex? He did the same thing."

As a leader, it would be prudent to have some degree of cultural competence. It is the X factor. If you want to understand Antoine, this detail must be calculated as you address him for good or challenging topics. You have to know Antoine came to you with nineteen or more years' worth of programming to think, act, and understand the world in a unique kind of way. Not only that, but Antoine also has several assumptions about you.

You see, around your own table, *and* since you were young, you are guaranteed to have had a starkly different conversation. And for some of you, the exhortations were completely opposite. And because of this, you understand Antoine's body language only the way your experience will allow. How many times could you be wrong about him? How many times *were* you wrong about his body language? And even more importantly, how many times did you take action based on it? You did because he did not *look* remorseful, or they didn't *seem* to care, or they *appeared* to be combative; and even worse, they *looked* guilty of what you accused them of.

Antoine sees the world so much differently than you probably do. And to be honest, there are many more that look like Antoine but see life even differently than he. As leaders, we talk about treating people the same. But treating people the same *is* the dilemma. Other than the standards of work, Antoine's needs should be handled as an individual. When or if he violates performance or ethical standards, you will have to address them judiciously. But understanding the mitigating factors will help you understand causal elements and corrective actions. It will be *why* Antoine missed the mark, performed poorly, or communicated unpredictably that should drive your corrective actions, not just because he did. It will be *why* Antoine succeeded, supported the team, and has a positive attitude that encourages you to recommend him for promotion.

HOW EASY WOULD IT BE TO ASK WHAT THOSE NONVERBALS MEAN?

The leadership lesson here is that our assumptions often fool us. As a leader, you have a responsibility to get their *own* words to speak for the nonverbals because you don't have a memorable list of ideas, nor does one exist, that are associated with any one particular demographic. I am often in the habit of asking, "What does that smirk mean?" or, "What does your silence mean?" or saying, "Tell me what you are thinking." All of this to eliminate your assumptions of what *your* kitchen table conversations drilled into *you*. This lesson is important because, as a leader, you will invariably address your people when they miss the mark. And you only get one chance to get this right before you potentially change Antoine's professional fate.

Trust me, it is *not* just Antoine, and it's *not* just one demographic. They *all* had a kitchen table experience, and they came to you with certain rules of life. Let us just openly admit we have no earthly idea which of our people are carrying some terrific emotional baggage at any point in time. I would predict the number is greater than an arbitrary 90 percent. So *their* rules to life are not wrong; they are just different. And more times than not, *yours* will likely not be in complete alignment. That is when you have to start asking questions—lots of them.

Cultural competence is this unique ability to understand, communicate with, and effectively interact with people across cultures. This X factor is the aggregate of one's own awareness, attitudes, and understanding of cultural differences. The degree of aptitude fairs low to high on a competence spectrum. In order to shift to the right on the spectrum, it must be done by this:

- – learn about yourself (self-aware)
- – learn about different cultures
- – interact with diverse groups
- – attend diversity-focused learning events

Antoine deserves a leader who is keenly aware that his life experience is different to some degree than yours. He deserves a leader who has an understanding of what happens at kitchen tables. He deserves a leader who will have Antoine's own words assigned to his nonverbals. He deserves a leader who will never act on assumptions. And if you want to influence optimal performance with your team and across your organization, it is time that you raise your cultural competence quotient to be the leader Antoine and every other worker needs.

Do me a favor and not limit this lesson to race. Also, do not restrict this lesson to the negative engagements with people like Antoine. Indeed, assumptions about seemingly *positive* nonverbals can be misread just as much. Leaders with the X factor of cultural competence are a game-changer for their people. When it is learned and felt, you will indeed influence optimal performance and retain your top talent. Do not forget: people do not quit their jobs; they quit their bosses.

So what happens if we were to uncover the topic of cultural competence? What if you made this a part of your leadership development? The fact is that leaders would be more tooled to face this problematic scenario with grace and consider of all the factors that employees like Antoine deal with on a regular basis. And even if there was no formal training on social structure, leaders should seek awareness, adjust their attitude toward it, and adapt their skills to confront these circumstances with compassion. There are opportunities here to formally or informally orient your midlevel management who have the lion share of responsibility to frontline employees. If we could simply change the culture from the middle, we can effectively build the environment where all our people have a chance to succeed.

CHANGING THE CULTURE FROM THE MIDDLE

While we are talking about culture, we might as well talk about shifting a culture. To be clear, understanding Antoine is much about the topic of competence in culture, and changing culture is absolutely about transforming the ideas or norms and the social systems. As far back as I can remember, it was a rule to never use the urinal directly next to another user—unless, of course, you are forced. I don't believe or remember if I was formally instructed to. There was no carrot nor stick; you just complied. Even today men frown on anyone violating the "code." As you can see, it does not take much to be introduced to a culture or norm. Once you see the vast majority of the in-group abiding, you simply follow suit.

So what does it take to shift the culture? Quite honestly, it takes influential people doing that "one thing" over and over again until it sticks. The time frame is almost never immediate. In fact, studies show it takes two to eight years for it to establish itself as a norm. In my experience, culture freezes are not a top-down approach. You would probably agree that top-down is not the ideal method to freeze a culture. It will likely only breed minimal compliance rather than commitment.

Man space in a urinal is hardly the culture shift we need to worry about in the workplace. There are significant ones, like encouraging horizontal communication structures, subordinate-initiated feedback, or even elimination of performance rating scales. These all have to be introduced by management. If culture freezes are not effectual from top-down, then these kinds of cultural shifts must be sprouting from the middle. That would mean the nucleus of cultural shifts, even when introduced top-down, can only be successful if actuated from the middle. That also means cultural shifts find their genesis in the middle, where they are deliberated and find oxygen. So it is at the midmanagement level, where the influencers roam, a culture that gives peer-to-peer performance feedback, a culture that everyone clocks out together, or a culture that establishes employee-nominating awards programs are given a platform to yield a strong organizational climate. It is management working with influencers that bet against the odds, take a stance, and risk a long, vulnerable change process to establish norms relevant to the organization. In the end, the entire organization and its people need to benefit and drive performance to its optimal levels. If you really want to influence a culture change, your influential leaders must:

1. Establish a purpose and feel a need for change.
2. Create an emotional connection and make it personal.
3. Model the behavior you want to be the norm.
4. Reinforce the culture.
5. Be patient! It takes time.

So why does this matter? Because leaders, even in the middle, are acting as the thermometer and the thermostat. As a thermometer, leaders often come into an organization and sense if members have or have not bonded with the group. As a thermostat, they have a primary responsibility to engage, motivate, and organize the team.

So it is on you to establish or shift the culture, even if it requires an influential vehicle to drive its change. I would start by seeking out the influencers to gain some momentum and finish with publicly rewarding those who have bought in. It may be unfair to correlate urinal man space and organizational culture. But I have overheard, more times than I can remember, a guy facing a urinal, look over and say, "You're breaking the code, man," followed by, "Move over!"

Again, in a global environment in which the people you lead will have diverse backgrounds, carrying the X factor should be the most sought after competency. Cultural competence requires that organizations have a defined set of values and principles, and demonstrate behaviors, attitudes, policies, and perspectives that enable them to work effectively cross culturally. Lack of cultural competence in the business community can damage an individual's self-esteem and career; but the unobservable psychological impact on the victims can go largely unnoticed until the threat of a class action suit brings them to light. Competent leaders consider how the woven norms create a social system that is inclusive. There are so many layers to cultural competence, but the X factor begins with acknowledging the differences. That alone will be a giant leap forward. Understanding their primary influence's role in instilling certain values will make you more compassionate to their perspective. Secondary influences, such as school systems, judicial systems, or political systems, all play a role in shaping the individual you are trying to develop today. And depending on how poorly or effectively those influences impacted the person will determine how considerate you will have to be for their assimilation to the team. This point is crucial. Primary influences are deeply rooted and virtually impossible to untangle. If I were you, I would not try to invalidate someone's truths with words. Those truths are wedged in and will be extremely difficult, if not impossible, to refute. But their *exposure* to different value systems, approaches to problem-solving, and ways to behave will shift their thinking about how they see the world. Refuting one's thinking with even a compelling argument is a shallow approach and will end up being short lived. But experiential learning will change a person for a lifetime. A culturally competent leader understands this dynamic, merges this skill into their overall leadership approach, and generates performance outcomes from traditionally marginalized individuals when others cannot. The X factor is the one skill that becomes the difference maker in establishing trust and influencing optimal performance in *all* your people.

CHAPTER 8

THE CURIOUS QUESTION OF WHY

FRIEDRICH WILHELM AUGUST HEINRICH FERDINAND Steuben, who died on November 28, 1794, was also referred to as Baron von Steuben. He was a Prussian and later an American military officer. He served as inspector general and a major general of the Continental Army during the American Revolutionary War at the request of George Washington. He was one of the fathers of the Continental Army for the purpose of teaching soldiers the essentials of military drills, tactics, and discipline. He wrote *Regulations for the Order and Discipline of the Troops of the United States* (1779), the book that served as the army's drill manual for decades. He became the architect of how military formations are presented in columns of four, marching in unison, and by cadence. Washington desperately needed help to develop a professional army. According to Washington, "They were a wreck."

Von Steuben was used to European soldiers who rarely questioned orders. Over time, von Steuben grew frustrated and wrote about his experience in his personal diary the following entry: "In Europe, you say to your soldier, 'Do this' and he does it. But I am obliged to say to the American, 'This is why you ought to do this,' and only then does he do it."

This question of why has become the pièce de résistance. And if you ask of the lineage from that of your predecessors, many would say, "This new generation is *so soft*. They are constantly asking why?" Well, I am presenting you a case that why is *not* a new challenge, and it extends back to the eighteenth century in American culture. It remains a serious leadership challenge going back to our founding. Do you think the need for influential leadership was different then than today? Absolutely not. In fact, it was noted that von Steuben had admonished his commissioned officers by saying, "You *must* tell the soldiers why."

I visited the Valley Forge site myself. It is about twenty miles northwest of Philadelphia. Since the war, the fort has been kept in remarkable shape by the National Park Service. The conservationists rebuilt and restored the thirty-five-hundred-square-mile area to pristine condition. You could feel the struggle that this ragtag group of militiamen of the Revolutionary War experienced at this particular site of eight winter encampments of the Continental Army. Standing in one of the tightly enclosed quarters that slept twelve but was spontaneously retrofitted for twenty or more, you could sense their frustration with the progress of the war. Lack of training, medicine, shortages of weapons, and protective clothing suitable to brave the winters caused soldiers to complain early and often. You can only imagine the soldiers repeating, "What is this all for?" or "Why am I subjecting myself to these conditions?"

Somehow we treat the question of why as a form of disrespect. In a verbal exchange, the leader apparently gets offended when the follower questions the necessity or the purpose of their directives. For some reason, leaders look at this query with disdain. I would speculate that, most certainly, it is because it is perceived as a challenge to one's authority, or a threat to a leader's decision-making, or a jab at one's ego. But regardless, the question must be entertained and given an appropriate response. But if this was addressed by General von Steuben back then, why are we still debating it today?

I would argue that why is a *particularly important* question. In fact, it probably needs to be addressed during the delivery of the directive. It would clear up elements of purpose, urgency, benefits, and strategy. It would bring the team all-in on the effort. Just think if you included the why *with* your directive. Your team would execute autonomously with fidelity, confidence, and purpose. It is obvious that the resistance to further instruction does displace a leader from their safe space of authority. A delivery of deeper analysis to your people does require an activation of your courage, credibility, collaboration, or character. It is a level up from leading by authority.

From my experience, following orders always seemed like a take-it-or-leave-it type of scenario. They called it "shut up and color." In other words, "Just do as I say." That *was* the culture of the time. And I can imagine, unapologetically, leaders believed that was the best method of getting the job done. In fact, our predecessors even believed their succeeding generations are simply *too soft* by straying from this cultural mindset. What could be so specious about communicating the purpose, the urgency, the benefits, or the strategy? I would suspect you are guaranteed to gain many more immediate supporters by taking the short time of offering context to the orders you expect the soldiers to lay their lives on the line for.

I would also offer that "do what you're told!" is an upside-down approach, just like it was in the eighteenth century. By continuing this mindset, innovation is skirted, learning and development are bypassed, and ideas are squashed. Today we need all those elements in a fast-paced, information-dominant decision space to be the most productive, most efficient, least wasteful, and lowest cost operationally. As a leader, we have to shed the conventional wisdom of the past and include *the why* as part of the directive *and* do it upfront. Responding to why upfront looks like this:

1. Here is the situation ...
2. This is how it can be mitigated ...
3. If we do nothing, this is what will happen ...
4. I am open to your ideas ...
5. I would like you to do ...

There are a number of leaders who still maintain a philosophy of power and control. They exercise their legitimate authority by rationalizing this is the way to ensure the work gets done in a precise time and manner in which they direct it. Power and control is an addictive position. I would argue there is a sociopathy to power in that it ruses one's own vulnerabilities, inadequacies, or esteem. It is a generational philosophy that was based on being a master to slaves, the man of the house, and single owner of a business. For the era, I can grasp the concept. In today's global work environment where diversity of thinking, women in the workforce, freedom to work, and unbridled civil rights, this generational philosophy is beyond archaic. Profitable organizations have found strength in speaking *truth to power* and exercising empowerment as the catapult to Fortune 500.

The need for influential leadership was the same then as it is today.

If we want to be better, smarter, and faster, leaders need to build-in *the why* as part of their directives and instructions. Yes, I mean at the same time. And even more importantly, leaders have to shift their attitude that these queries are not an inquisition, not a personal offense, or not an attack on their authority. I would offer that leaders actually *need* followers to ask why. It compels the leader to challenge their own logic and *simply* reason with others. It forces them to examine the policy from which they direct. After all, leading beyond your legitimate authority—as addressed in chapter 3, "The Safe Space of Leading by Authority"—will suppress those autocratic approaches, which is often comfortably disguised as sound leadership.

CALLING GENERATION X

Today we are constantly pointing the finger at millennials and Generation Zs because they absolutely *have* to be the problem with our culture and certainly attribute the question of why to them. The usual complaints are they are far too lazy, disloyal, reclusive, and selfish. Studies have shown that many of those attributes are accurate. But the same studies show that they are also incredibly brilliant, multi-talented, purpose-driven, and work efficiently in teams. And with all that, I can see multitudes of ways to inspire them. But there is one key fact that must be understood. Gen Z maintains a distain for traditional hierarchies. And because of this, as a whole, they do not trust traditional company norms, bureaucracies, military structures, or government institutions. For some reason, we have marked this generation as one that has flipped its lid.

On the other hand, Gen X is so regimented that they share this contempt for the millennial's freestyle mode. They have been taught to stay in your box, color inside the lines, and be disciplined and self-sufficient, even though they did not like the rigid lifestyle themselves. This is an incredible contrast to its successors but, even still, offers a challenge to inspire their offspring. So what is wrong with you, X? You are talented and resourceful with a tremendous amount of leadership acumen. Have you given up? Is the challenge too difficult?

Generation identification has been going on since only the 1990s. Generation identification is *not* an official recognized naming convention. It was initially introduced to the mainstream by television personality Tom Brokaw when he named the citizens of the World War II era, who were born between 1901 and 1927, as the Greatest Generation. After that, they introduced cohorts of different eras, such as the baby boomers, Generation X, millennials, Gen Z, and now Generation Alpha. Alphas are those born in 2010 through what will be the mid-2020s. Largely a media and advertising campaign, however, social scientists have been studying these demographic cohorts for generational norms and structure for understanding their strengths, weaknesses, behaviors, and practices. There are obvious societal norms that accompany these generations with direct correlations to the economy, education, shifting family structure, access to information, gender orientation endorsement, mortality rates, and the remarkable rise in technology making the globe shrink in its virtual size. With each cohort, scientists have found some behavioral norms and qualities transitioned from generation to generation but also altered to meeting the demands of changing societies. It goes without saying that identification with a generational cohort does not box you in. Many bridge one generational identification to the other based on the new generational migration or their saturated influence from the previous generation.

Just think if you conflated emotional intelligence, this squishy quality said to be only for the weak, with your instinctive qualities to lead. Just think if you married empathy and resourcefulness to show Z how to overcome their own societal challenges. Just think if used your adaptive traits to motivate this challenging societal shift. Or would you rather fold your arms and point at the weakness of, quite honestly, the people *you* created with helicopter parenting styles, rewarding mediocre performance, and bullying? The point is there are tremendous opportunities here to extract from your own innate strengths to lead and inspire the latest generations.

For X to lead in this environment, you have to set aside those biases that cast others as the enemy of our culture. Be resourceful enough to build on the talents and instincts of the new occupants of the workforce. And if you are really the superior generation than that of your spawn, this is your call to lead. If Gen Z distrusts traditional hierarchies, then building trust and relinquishing autonomy, and giving your people a voice will counteract those inclinations of this youthful generation. If they have a predisposition to perform better in groups, do not force a top-down, traditionalist structure to only marginalize their tendencies. Yes, this will alter your leadership style. Yes, you will approach leadership in a different way. Yes, this will make you a bit uncomfortable. But the prospects of spurring along their attributes will yield gains that your current generation could never.

With the challenges we are facing today, I offer an approach that is in Gen X's wheelhouse: (1) Find the issues that really are a thorn—kill them on the spot; (2) Identify the gaps where the company has not weighed in—fill it; (3) be present and visible—get your boots dirty; (4) be the coach on the field by putting the right players on the field at the right time; take the right players off the field at the right time; and *for God's sake* call time-out when it is time to take a knee and adjust your approaches.

We have been led to believe that why is a brand-new *challenge* of our new generations—it is not. But it could certainly be a sociological dilemma that challenges your philosophy on leading people. The time committed to being responsive to your people will pay dividends in more than one way. If why is such an issue for you, you have to get down to the essence of the matter. Usually, there is an iceberg. You know, the issues that lay beneath the surface that are not obvious to you or anyone else. Often it is trivialized or dismissed as something completely different. You can spot icebergs when a person overreacts to an issue that does not correspond with the seriousness of the problem. But when the iceberg is revealed, you can find exactly what issue is and why you struggle with it.

As leaders, we have juggled the issue of generation shaming and the blame game for quite some time now. We have pointed and criticized. But the one thing we have not done is owned the circumstances, got ahead of the issue, and found improved methods to communicate in an effort to build commitment. We also have not identified the strengths our people. And because their behavior is foreign to your societal norms, you denigrate it as the root to poor performance. Phrases like, "This is how we have always done it" is only said to protect you from leading differently. Allowing past cultural norms to determine how we communicate or behave today, when you look at it, borders on the spectrum of insanity. It is time to let go of the bell-bottoms era of effective communication. There is an old saying that says, "Get over yourself!" Indeed, it is time.

General von Steuben had clearly addressed why and made a cogent argument of why we should tolerate this line of questioning in the eighteenth century. When you think about it, why is more of a challenge for the leader than it is the indiscipline of the subordinate. To your people, why is an obvious appeal. When it is countered negatively, there is a degree of resentment and even bewilderment to why the leader is opposed to responding. You have to admit, it is a little ridiculous. Standing your ground by fighting a response is simply a reflection of the strength of your self-esteem. Instead of being combative, we can make this struggle a thing of the past.

CHAPTER 9

WHAT IS IT ABOUT EMPATHY?

WHY CAN'T THEY JUST DO the work without inserting their personal drama into the situation? You are running a place of business, not a social services clinic, right?

You have seen these scenarios. While you are at work, you see one of your people looking disheveled, and you naturally ask, "What's wrong?" Then they unload on you that their child, spouse, friend, or parent is in poor medical condition. As they pause to cry, you say, "You will be OK," and wander off. Sound familiar? Then there are also times when you will see one of you people struggling to perform. When asked about any difficulties they are experiencing, they share that they are getting a divorce and are a little distracted. Of course, depending your marital or relationship experience, you may have very little to offer. So you finish with, "Sorry to hear that," and wander off again.

What is it about this empathy thing that leaders fail to express it? There is probably an endless number of reasons why supervisors fail to demonstrate this relational gift. Some believe empathy simply does not belong in the workplace. And no fault of their own; some just were not nurtured to show it. I am sure some have difficulty dealing with their employees' pain because it makes them feel hurt themselves. And some fear fumbling an uncomfortable conversation and inadvertently making it worse. I would bet that the majority of people who have difficulty expressing empathy find it hard to match, on the fly, the emotional wavelength of the other. And when your body language is called for you to make the adjustment, your mind cannot make the shift in time to appear authentic. Then you fumble the experience and make matters worse. That ends up being an awkward and vulnerable space to be in that many leaders are not ready for.

Oftentimes I hear leaders say, "I don't have time for that." Or they say, "What does that have to do with me?" Of course, when one of your people comes to you with, "Do you have a minute?" you will have to set aside some time to listen and respond. What does that have to do with you? From my perspective, *it has everything to do with you*. Because if you are in the business of influencing optimal performance, your response will change not only what happens to this person, it will signal your position on people-issues to the entire team. So you have to be sure what you are unconsciously communicating. Because getting the best out of your people at work requires that you treat them *like people*. And people need this granular level of social interaction, as the workplace takes a third of their lives, as it does yours.

Here's the thing: It is easy to get caught up in assigning an employee ID number to your people and forget they are living, breathing beings. You have a job to do, and they can unintentionally throw a wrench at achieving team goals or meeting deadlines. Addressing unanticipated issues with dignity and respect will close the gap between what *they expect* of you and what you actually do. Ultimately, they do not want to be treated like a number. And if you do, you can bet they will be defiant and will never align with what you are trying to get done. In fairness to fast pace organizations, it is easy to fall in the trap of overlooking the humanity of the people who carry out the work. In these environments, each of them are being stalked by computer systems in an effort to track their productivity. They are placed in an assembly line formation, and they perform repetitive motions or actions. Then, when bells and sounds direct them to start and stop, the environment and activity blurs your mind to diminish their humanness. Evidence of this can be seen when an employee gets hurt, and the leader focuses on their replacement in the systematic cog rather than their interest in the health and safety of the individual. The trap is deceiving when you are deep in systematic process. Leaders who can extricate themselves from the chain and sprocket of the business will find it easier to adjust to the emotional wavelengths of their people.

LILIANA

Liliana is a department supervisor for a high-paced production company. She started with the company as a Level 1 craft employee. She has now been there for eighteen years. Liliana, during her early years, was among the hardest working and most productive employees in the office and maybe even in the entire District. I forgot to say, she speaks English as a second language and has a rather strong accent, even though she speaks English perfectly. She lacks confidence in her ability to communicate to her people because of her perceived communication barriers. Liliana sees having a well-paying and stable job as a success story. And because of that, she works like her life depends on it every single day—even to the point she struggles with work-life balance. After ten years with the company, Liliana's supervisor took a chance on her and brought her up to be a shift manager. Even though Liliana had reservations about filling such a role, she flourished. As she began to develop her newfound leadership skills as a shift manager, Liliana would begin to push the craft employees hard to meet the productivity goals of the office. Liliana suffered no fools and took each challenge head-on. She was the perfect shift manager to meet the fluctuating demands of the job and the metrics showed. Liliana relocated four times in her position as manager. Every time, she was the top producer. Her confidence was high but there was one thing that would give her fits. She felt that employees should share her work ethic and should leave their personal drama at home—you came here to work. Eventually, Liliana would get promoted twice more to supervisor, where she brought her productivity talents to the next level. The problem with Liliana was that she became hardened by the number of excuses that malingering employees presented her on a daily basis. She finally came to a point where she no longer was listening.

One day Darlene came to Liliana with an issue that was a soft spot for her. Darlene tended to have *several* soft spots but this time it was serious. Darlene was an unreliable employee. When things did not go her way, she would go to the union or raise EEO complaint. Liliana had already had it up to here when it came to Darlene, and this time she was not having it. "Liliana, my dog died." Because Liliana did not have dogs, nor wanted pets, she did not sense the gravity of the issue. Liliana replied with, "I hope you bury it on your day off because we need you here." Darlene was so upset that she stormed out of the building. Liliana stood there with her hands on her hips, watching Darlene from the glass door. For the life of her, Liliana could not understand why Darlene was so upset.

Empathy is *not* sympathy. It is a learned behavior to help you *show up* for other people when they need it most. It is not a have or do not have. Empathy is a willingness to connect on the other's emotional wavelength to see the situation through their eyes. It is willing to connect, willing to feel, and willing to take action. In a supervisor-employee relationship, the employee is looking to you to perceive their emotion and support them. I would venture to say employees *expect* you to respond with empathy. And when you do not, they are deeply troubled by it.

Accommodating everyone's needs is not realistic. But I am pretty certain you can pull from the empathy organ inside of you and make a reasonable settlement that doesn't slow production or brings business to a halt. I'm pregnant, I'm hot, I'm cold, I need Tuesday's off, my kid gets home at three, or "Is there any way that you can (fill in the blank)." You can best believe, in more cases than you have chosen against, the answer could have been, "Yes!" When you do, you may have won them over for a lifetime.

> ## "I CAN'T DO THAT FOR YOU, OR I'LL HAVE TO DO IT FOR EVERYONE."

Empathy is sometimes also, "Sorry, I understand this is a tough predicament for you, but I have looked into it, and I cannot accommodate this for you. And in fact, you are probably going to experience more of this, so I'm going to ask that you shift things around on your part to make this work." Here is the key part that works in this response, "I looked into it." Responding by saying sorry; that's too bad; you'll be fine; or I can't do that for you, or I'll have to do it for everyone will wedge distance between yourself and your team. So *look into it* before you respond. As you judge the situation against the risk to operations, your decision will affect their current circumstance and then unconsciously for all other matters for the duration of your leader-employee relationship.

- – Listen—don't judge.
- – Understand their perspective.
- – Assess the risk to operations.
- – Communicate with care.

My point is that empathy is more about *you* than it is your employees' circumstances. It is about how *you* value relationships. Empathy is about *you* being emotional enough, connected enough, and compassionate enough to consider the person's difficulty versus the risk to operations. Being empathetic may even expose your own vulnerabilities. You may even have a feeling of appearing weak by being willing to put the work of one on the backs of others. And I will assume you will not want to conflate work and personal matters. But there is a real opportunity here to empower, help, and retain a proud employee at their point of need.

Liliana missed a real opportunity there. And I bet you are thinking, *It is what it is* when it comes to Liliana's empathy organ, but I disagree. People who lack empathy are *not* a lost cause. It is actually the opposite if, of course, you are willing to work on it. Other than being raised in a low empathy circle, there are a few factors that lend toward being low on the meter. Typically, if you fit the modus operandi of being less empathetic, you probably have established a rigid worldview about people. You see people as homogenous and likely have surrounded yourself with those who are much like you. The cure is being open to learning about others, putting yourself in other's circumstances, or even working in shared causes that forces you connect to contrasting situations you would not normally find yourself in. Liliana will not realize she is low on the empathy meter until she is tapped with the wand of self-awareness. Then it will be up to her.

BARBARA

Do you know Barbara? Of course you do. Everyone knows Barbara. Barbara is the one when anyone brings up her name you spot facial expression and body language changes. Barbara is your daily challenge. She does the work, but it comes with an amazing amount of emotional commentary. You know there will always be Barbaras on your team and in your organization who are difficult to manage. As their leader, your goal is to handle them with grace and kindness. Of course, that is much easier said than done. But in the end, you have the responsibility to lead and inspire a cohesive and functioning team. And just like every other environment, the Pareto principle will always kick in, and you will tend to spend 80 percent of your time on 20 percent of your problems or distractions. When this happens, you will have to recognize it and make a business-level decision—keep her or terminate her.

There are two types of Barbaras: One who is exceptionally difficult to work with and is an average or below-average performer. Or the other, she complains of just about everything, disguising it as playful banter. But regardless, it is all a distraction. And every minute you spend responding to Barbara is one additional minute of unproductive work. Sending Barbara back to her cubicle, workstation, or toolbox is a temporary fix. She will back—she will *always* be back. At some point, you will have to uncover the underlying issues.

Here is the other side of the story: Difficult people have icebergs like everyone else. And almost always there is a history behind the awkwardness, complaints, and banter. If you intend to keep her on the team, you will have to get to the bottom of it and then hold her accountable. Icebergs are the emotional baggage that lay below the surface and manifests itself by low-level drama that does not match the matters before you. You really have to listen for it. In some cases you will have to employ root causal techniques to uncover them.

MORALE = PRODUCTIVITY = GOAL ACCOMPLISHMENT

But there is one more piece to this puzzle. Barbara is not just a distraction to the leader; she is also a frustration to her coworkers. And certainly, if she is not carrying her own productive weight, you will have a silent and growing bitterness that will brew until it explodes by one or more of her peers. It sounds like, "Why do they let her get away with this?" The team just wants you to act, especially if they find themselves covering for her. And if you do not act, you will begin to lose respect, credibility, and trust with your team.

So here you are, in the middle of the difficult space between people and production—yep, that is you! You were put in this position to achieve the bottom line: profits, performance, and mission. So, if there are any barriers, to that end, they must be addressed. At the same time, you have a responsibility to lead, develop, and influence individuals and the team to optimal performance. It is a fine balance that comes with listening, responding with empathy, reacting with self-control, and having bias to act. You simply cannot sacrifice production to deal with Barbara. But you absolutely cannot ignore or dismiss her either.

WITH DIFFICULT PEOPLE:

- Do not feed into them.
- Do not prolong your exposure to them.
- Listen for icebergs.
- Draw a clear redline.
- Help them remove their barriers.
- Above all, do not let them get you down—or everybody else.

The bottom line: empathy *obviously* has a role in your leadership style and should take a central position in your communication and engagement. Do not allow it to be summed up as tears and hugs. Empathy is hardly that. It is more of a relational *gift* that must be understood and tuned into. Some have fears of missing the connection and saying or doing something that makes matters worse. Some do not value its effect. And some believe being empathetic makes you too vulnerable as a leader. Of course, it is your vulnerability where trust and connections are established. Drawing from your empathy capacity will not show weakness; it will do the opposite. It will actually highlight your leadership maturity. Deciding on how to act will be *entirely* up to you. And however you respond, they want to know you cared to understand. If the saying, "People do not quit their jobs; they quit their bosses" or the saying, "People will forget the things you did, but they won't forget how you made them feel" are true, then how you link up to their emotional signature for whatever topic will be a difference maker in the success of the organization. Just remember, the people chose you to share their good or bad news—they chose *you*. And when that is the case, you will have to show up for them. Show up with an active-constructive response. The kind of response that confirms the trust, values the relationship, and gives the feeling of validation. Even if you do not believe in the topic, it will not ever matter. What will matter is how they felt walking away from the exchange. Finally, in the exchange, unusual requests will be hinted to that you would typically refuse without considerable thought. But with a bias for empathy, there may be opportunities to get to "Yes." And when you do, you will have influenced optimal performance for that individual and the whole team.

Leaders: "Do you have a minute?"

[THE FORMULA]

www.extracttheleader.com

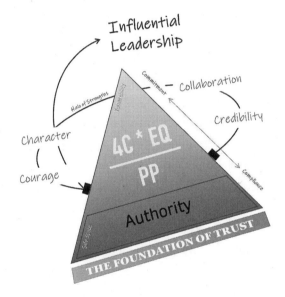

https://one57nine.com/the-foundation

THE FORMULA TO INFLUENCING OPTIMAL PERFORMANCE

The strongest *and most fragile* source of leadership power is born from personal power (also called reverent power). This type of power is not given to you by your bosses. Rather, it is *granted* to you by your followers. It is the thrust of your influence. Let us tease out how personal power is the formula to influential leadership:

Authority. The power or right to give orders, make decisions, and enforce obedience.

Influence. The capacity to have an effect on the character, development, or behavior of someone or something, or the effect itself.

Influence comes from your personal power (PP). But personal power alone is fleeting. It must accompany other sources of power—that is, connection, information, reward, coercive, etc. Your followers grant to you your personal power. The other sources of power are established by superiors or an authority. It is arguably the toughest power to obtain because it is emotional and irrational among humans. Personal power stems from trust that only comes from relationship building.

How do I dial in in my personal power?

Here is my take: Personal power is gained from being authentic. Those who wield a heavy amount of personal power are confident, vulnerable, and empathetic. They are heavy communicators and share information when they know it. Most people who have a tremendous amount of personal power are optimists, but it is not compulsory. Followers who grant personal power connect with their leader's values. There is an incredible amount of trust that is freely granted. They feel comfortable with their personally set boundaries, which are relative to that individual relationship. Those with personal power have also established themselves with expertise or experience in their fields. They have a reputation for their willingness to assist others. And finally, they secure wins for the team.

Personal power underpins effective leadership qualities.

Lead with *my* four Cs:

Character. The strength and originality in a person's nature. A person's good reputation.

Competence. The ability to do something successfully or efficiently.

Courage. The quality or state of having or showing mental or moral strength to face danger, fear, or difficulty.

Collaborate. To work jointly on an activity, especially to produce or create something.

Lead with EQ:

Emotional Intelligence (EQ). The degree in which one is aware of, controls, and expresses one's emotions, handles interpersonal relationships judiciously and with empathy.

$$\frac{4C * EQ}{PP}$$

[THE BACK NINE]

CHAPTER 10

MISMANAGEMENT OF THE STORMING PHASE

THERE IS ONE THING THAT is certain. When humans gather, it is just a matter of time before there will be conflict. It is not *if* there will be conflict; it is when. Dealing with conflict is not one of those skills that is taught. For most, it happens to be experiential. As it would have it, companies don't get to be protected from it. So not only are leaders focused on meeting business objectives, but they also have a parallel responsibility to bring their people together and officiate the drama to form a cohesive team. And regardless of the organizational design, cultivating a team and setting them on the right foot rests solely on the leader. I know—sometimes you will hear that because they are all adults each member is responsible for themself. But just like there is one set of hands on a steering wheel, so, too, is it the leader's responsibility for the direction of the team. There is no doubt that steering a team will be a difficult task, and there is a guarantee to be bumps in the road. Think about a time when you were put in the position to lead a newly constructed team. Some of you may or may not have participated in this kind of exercise. If you have not, keep in mind there is a phase in group development that is generally mismanaged. I am highlighting it now so you will be aware when you are confronted with it. It not only occurs in business, but you will see it also in the building of private organizations, process improvement teams, church choirs, and even in newly blended families. You will see it also in new operations, incorporated support functions, or new layers in management as well. You will have to be ready to recognize it. Any basic leadership course will emphasize group development, sometimes called group dynamics, and their four distinct phases:

- forming
- storming
- norming
- performing

For this chapter, I am going to skip ahead to storming, as it is aptly named. In my experience, I have seen members of the team exhibit uncontrollable tensions with other members of the group. I am sure you have seen it yourself. One member is giving another the business for one reason or another. And more subtly, you have even seen some members scanning the professional bios of others so they can compare how they measure up with their perceived rival. This storming stage is marked by competition and conflict. Here individuals begin low-level undercutting, which is detected often by sarcasm, eye rolling, and mumbling, all in an effort to solidify a desirable role within the group. You can even spot low-key power struggles by a member overcontributing to meaningless topics or soliciting cosigners to their agendas. When the group is dismissed, and they go their own ways, cliques congeal in hallways and parking lots to discuss how they see things developing. Oddly, those contributions were not raised in the group at large and could have potentially added value to the effort. It is probably the most stressful time in the group's development.

Group development is the process in which a team is formed *and* sustained through its maturation. Every group is constantly navigating through one phase or another at some point in time. Even well-established teams and organizations progress through phases. And some groups struggle and remain stagnant in certain phases. There are others that proceed to an esprit stage, where the performance activity uncovers an additional gear, and the dynamics of team are now based on integrity, trust, teamwork, humility, and communication.

COMMAND POST

The command post is an executive agency that works directly for the military commander of a base. The agency exists to carry out the operational directions of the commander to support a population of eight to ten thousand military professionals and set the conditions for their safety, security, and the defense of the base in times of peace and war. The command post is typically composed of fifteen to twenty operations controllers who maintain top secret clearances so they can access and decipher Pentagon-level emergency conditions. As you would bet, these are pretty reliable and intelligent people who stand the watch on a twenty-four-hour cycle to guarantee those conditions are ready to execute and protect the population. During the shift, the operations controllers will monitor and give direction to a variety of aircraft arriving and departing and synchronize assistance to the pilots and ground support teams that ready airplanes for their next missions.

As you would suspect, there is a tremendous amount of drama in these places because of the number hours and isolation by a group of young controllers remanded to their stations in a bunker-like environment. When I arrived at this command post as their new leader and a newly trained controller, I got the full leadership experience. In my first week, they did not hold back on all of the details of why they were underperforming and struggling to get along. I sat back and gathered the information so I could understand it for myself and began to put the pieces back together. But it was because I allowed the team to work out their issues and nudge them only with those unmovable challenges that they began to see cohesion. I even found myself threatening to have everyone work in a single room to stop the perceived favoritism. When Torrie arrived, I appointed him as the new operations manager. Torrie was obviously new to the team, but he had immediately won their respect. Torrie's outgoing personality and competitive attitude was exactly what they needed. Still, I had to leave high performers in charge over veteran controllers to improve our performance. That did not go over well with those who were passed over, but it did get us off the radar of poor performance. I even put a junior manager in charge of a rather important role. Finally, after getting back on our feet, we gained a transferred-in senior controller named Allen. Allen had some training gaps because he had been out of the field for several years. But he came in willing to learn and ready to lead. Unfortunately, his leadership skills were a bit lacking. I would classify Allen as a late bloomer—late to learn the job and late to develop as a leader. As we gradually and deliberately put him in a leadership role, you could see the team's performance begin to decline because the controllers began to take exception to Allen's behavior and approaches to leading. Again, I nudged the team back and encouraged Allen to lead in a way that motivates and inspires the team. Mo would come to me regularly and advised that I confront him about his behavior. Mo was one the team's star high performers and had been put in a leadership role ahead of her peers. But it was Torrie who took the initiative to help Allen assimilate with team. Because Torrie was his peer, he would give Allen valued feedback. He also would talk to each of the controllers and put them at ease. He had a way of doing that. The entire team admired Torrie because of his willingness to empower, encourage, and innovate. Unfortunately, Allen had a dominant personality. Not only that, but he was also six foot two and roughly 240 pounds—he even looked intimidating. He would admit he was more of an autocratic type based on his experience because that was the old-school way. There was no doubt he made an effort to fit in with the team, but sometimes his comments and tactics turned people off. Allen was willing to do whatever was necessary, but he struggled with his personality fitting in with team. Eventually, I had to step in to reprimand Allen. But unless I felt Allen was mistreating the team, I would leave it up to them to adjust to Allen and his style as we also worked with him to be a better leader. Even though it is difficult to watch, it was important to send his people back to their stations and adjust to Allen's style. After all, not *everyone* will like their leader—you can bet on that. So it would be wrong of me to intervene and undercut him. Eventually, the team got back to raising the bar and exceeding organizational goals. Allen was not able to make the adjustment to win over the team, but the team got back to work and drama dissipated. The team figured out a way to adjust and transition to the norming phase. Because of the conflict, Torrie, Allen, Mo, and especially the team grew as individuals and as a group.

Why do I suppose leaders mismanage this? Principally, I believe leaders send the members to their own corners too prematurely.

This *is* the storming phase, and you should concede a level of stress and conflict. As the leader, you are, *or should have been*, deliberate in selecting the team members and their captains. So, allow the team to attune until they fit. By officiating the storming phase too strictly, the members may sequester their objections and disputes. Ultimately, it delays or effectively undermines the period of the storming phase. And in some cases, some teams never successfully progress through it. Avoid botching this step by giving the team members opportunities to work things out. Even toddlers find resolution in sandboxes. I am certain adults can too in the board room.

You can help facilitate a healthy storming by recognizing and bringing the individual issues to the surface and allow the team members to address them. Be cognizant of the nonverbals around the room. Those nonverbals have something to say. Of course, you do not want to get mired in relationship and emotional issues. The team still needs to be productive and actually perform the task. But skirting the storming is just as harmful. So resolve *only* the issues that cannot seem to be negotiated. Intervene *only* to find compromise when they have reached an impasse. But most importantly, establish as a nonnegotiable that the members maintain a high level of respect with and among the group.

Conflict is ironically the glue to long-established relationships. After the team survives a healthy and protracted conflict, it becomes the catalyst that launches a team forward. It is a natural clash of ideas that if you keep your ears open, there is a lesson to be learned from it. The growth that is developed through conflict is located in the individual and collective lessons where each learns of the roles, strategies, intentions, skills, or contributions. When team members validate the other member's inputs, trust begins to bring and keep the team together. And the opposite, when validation is not present, trust is absent and increased tension becomes the adhesive. Either way, the team is coming together by trust or friction. If you want the team to grow together allow healthy conflict to prevail. You will never have to search for cruel conflict; it will expose itself. Cruel conflict activates when those ideas and motives do not fit the strategy of the team. In the discourse, the conflict itself shines a light on those with bad intentions. Because when you sift through the noise, there is a selfish idea being put forth or an ulterior motive at play. Even still, the conflict will be the impetus to the cohesion as they navigate through the phases of group development.

It would be a failure on my part to gloss over the necessities to deconstruct a stalemate:

- Listen to each of the factions with all your senses. What are the facts?
- Ask questions to gain a full understanding of the perspectives.
- Allot opportunities for each to assert what response or direction solves the dilemma.
- Allow them to negotiate on what solves it permanently, with the best results, or the least collateral damage.

I realize watching the storming phase can be a bit uncomfortable. For some, it may even be unsettling. If you happen to be a brother or sister, you can easily relate. Even with continual disagreements, the strength of your sibling love is an example of how to manage a lifelong storming phase. Have you seen two unfamiliar dogs sniff each other? If you understand that familiarity process, there is nothing you can do to break it other than waiting it out. Ironically, dogs can *sniff* the mood of another dog. If they begin growling, you yank their chains.

Similarly, if your team cannot seem to progress through this phase, evaluate *your* criteria and *your* selection of the team's leader. Provide mentorship or offer coaching. Again, *you chose them.* Just know, every time you bring in a new member, and especially a leader into the group, there is a degree of sniffing or storming that will always occur. You will notice the closer the new member is to the top of the team's organization chart, the stronger the agitation will be.

WHAT AN UNCOMFORTABLE CONVERSATION SAYS ABOUT YOU

Eric was this kind of guy who when you first meet him, you could not help but smile. He had one of those personalities that, if you had never met him before, you would automatically like him—it probably was the southern charm. When Eric would steer you through his spaces, you would have a ton of confidence that his section was performing very well. Eric had a way of distracting you with his hospitality, but after you had been around the spaces a while longer, you would figure out that it was all smoke and mirrors. That was the thing. I could not put my finger on it, but there was just something missing. And after you got a chance to speak to the employees, it would all become clear.

Eric intended to talk to me about preparing him for promotion, but I had something different in mind. The grapevine falsely believed Eric was a shoo-in for the job. He absolutely thought that it was *his* time. After all, he was the senior person. The only thing, Eric was a pain in the ass toward his people. He was tough to work for and with. From all the feedback I was getting, they were miserable. But when Eric cosseted the visiting management teams and excessively underscored his apparent successes, they were sure he was on his way. Even with the overindulgence, you could see the gaps in his leadership through the morale of his people. Promoting him to the next level now would, quite honestly, be an absurdity. Eric thought he was clearly the best candidate for the job, and he could not fathom management selecting anyone else.

This is one of those times when a tough leadership conversation is needed and necessary. Conversations like these are certainly not limited to promotions. It can be about anything—team conflicts, performance, differences in opinion, or even results. These kinds of conversations come around often. In fact, you may face these daily. And to put it bluntly, when you avoid them, you become the problem because these uneasy conversations are inescapable. There is something about the human psyche that leaders abstain from these tough conversations. I can imagine for a number of reasons, but *not* having it is a far worse situation. How you handle it will show your growth as a leader and the strength of your emotional intelligence.

What is it about tough conversations that makes leaders avoid them? In this case, Eric needed someone to be honest with him. He needed someone to set the record straight. And most importantly, he needed to know what management was truly thinking. The tough part for the leader is the fear of an unknown escalation or maybe even losing your most senior worker. And just think if Eric was your most productive performer too. Then the conversation gets even more agonizing. Will that be enough to shy away? I know it will be tough to tell Eric that you will not be considering him. But if you do not, you could inadvertently deliver to your people a toxic leader. So you can see that your conflict avoidance has consequences and is an indictment on your courage and credibility.

I get it. Most people want to prevent arguments, so they avoid the subject altogether. There is a loose and subjective distinction between an argument and having a conversation, even if it is difficult. A conversation is more of an exchange of individual ideas between people, while an argument is a statement of perceived facts used to support a concept. Understanding this, there is certainly nothing wrong with an argument. It is how the argument is communicated, which often redefines it, and that changes its connotation. Attorneys can argue cases, doctors argue at boards, politicians argue ideas—make sense? Here is the thing: In the end, these exchanges always have to result in influencing optimal performance and putting the company in a better position. So make your argument on the relative facts. Regardless of the issue, however, the company's shareholder value and mission effectiveness must be at the heart of the issue.

Telling someone they are underperforming, their personality conflicts, their behavior is a risk, or you are passing on their new position is not always easy to communicate, but it has to be done by *you*. Because these discussions are avoided so much, people like Eric go on thinking they are the pick of the litter. And even more importantly, they may go on to terrorize the team in their new and more powerful role. For some, the idea of Eric wielding more power is a bit more than they can handle, so now you have members of your team transferring out, contemplating quitting, or submitting their resignations. Ultimately, the message has to be received, otherwise bad things happen. You owe your people an honest exchange. Picture this, how you handle an uncomfortable conversation can be the difference between it being a disciplinary session or a developmental opportunity.

> **AS THE LEADER, YOU OWN THE CONVERSATION.**

You can simplify these tough conversations in several ways. You can cut to the chase, lay it on them easy, or nest it between two positives in hopes they catch your drift. But here is what I would do:

- Observation: I observed your behavior ...
- Assessment: It impacted the operation ...
- Expectation: In the future, I expect you ...
- Prognosis: If you commit to this, we will consider ...

In my experience, relationships and employee engagement are vitally important here. How well you know your people takes the lack of trust off the table. But looked at differently, it also puts trust firmly on the table. Even though you simplify the conversation, it does not mean it will not become emotional. As the leader, it is absolutely your responsibility to steer the conversation. You own the exchange and its volume, its direction, its temperature, and especially its closing. No matter the situation, do not surrender it and do not allow it to be confiscated. Most importantly, you cannot allow the emotion of it all to bump you from your position—your position as leader and your position in the conversation. And for God's sake, never concede the moral high ground—ever (a line from my friend Tim "Chachi" Pachasa).

I was taught for many years that everything is a negotiation—everything. Since ultimately you want a positive outcome, negotiating with Eric and his performance is where you are striving to get to. Eric may have believed he had the upper hand because of his seniority and productivity. Those variables only matter if you make them matter. Your objective is to close the employee expectation gap with Eric, shift the perceptions into realities and to eliminate the noise that prevents his success. So, having this tough conversation is necessary and should be arbitrated. Getting past your own level of self-confidence, harboring conflicting values, or any other barriers will be the chasm that gets between having this successful dialogue. Plainly stated, the lack of comfort rests with you, and not with Eric. So now what has your uncomfortable conversations said about you?

One last thing: Your team's success matters to all stakeholders *and* to the team itself. Testing out the unchartered waters by allowing conflict to develop does stretch the team and their growth, but deliberately navigating them though those waters will show what *you* are made of. Picture the rowing crew team captain with a megaphone. They are constantly communicating the tempo. As a rower or two gets out of sync, the vocal cadence helps them adjust to the flow. The rowers put their heads down and have the trust and confidence in the captain's direction. Team success will always begin with trust, as you would expect. When the trust is established, accountability to the outcome will take center stage. Being accountable to each other sets guardrails on the collective efforts and assures its members will stay on course. Next, commitment is established when trust and accountability have congealed. The team is communicating and putting it first. There is a guarantee to have conflict. You should expect it. Conflict from the well-intended is a positive thing and should not be averted to save an argument. This is where the lessons are learned. The durability of a team is in its results. Results drive commitment to the process and each other. Moral victories, or coming up short, are good but are only short lived. They do galvanize the team for the next opportunity, but moral victories need to be backed up by a win at some point. The one thing about moral victories is that it reminds you of the conflict and assures you that you are progressing in the right direction. But a win will corral the team and indicate the conflict was well worth it. If you want to influence optimal performance, get comfortable with an uncomfortable storming phase. In the end, it will be worth it.

CHAPTER 11

DIAGNOSIS: BURNOUT

THE WORKPLACE PLAYS A KEY role in the livelihood of an individual. The reality is, you are likely to spend more time at the office than you will actually spend at your home. It is almost a guarantee that more than half of your friends will be met at work. And because of this, people want this environment to be as pleasant and enjoyable as their homes. It goes without saying—the workplace can be the key determinant of your social, economic, and now technological growth. But when going to the office feels like work, it can really wear on you. It has a tremendous impact on your consciousness, and it will manifest in your attitude as you walk through the doors. For the amount of time spent on the grind, a healthy work environment can surely make work more palatable. And just hopefully, it could actually be fun. It is fantastic to see a healthy organization perform at its optimal best. You may have seen it. They are communicating, sharing, taking work off each other's plates. They are bringing food from home to share, laughing in the break room, and scheduling off-duty get-togethers. They are taking the initiative, improving processes, cheering each other on, and celebrating wins. They are open to change, giving and receiving constructive criticism, and completely focused on the bottom line—achieve the shared organizational goals.

But have you ever seen how a team signals they are burnt out? I would bet you have. But oftentimes leaders overlook, misread, or *outright ignore* this organizational condition. The signals are blatantly obvious. Because if you can identify when they are performing at their optimal best, how could you miss when they are not? Short of your employees simply quitting, burnout comes in these forms:

- sarcasm that is voiced at the end of conversations, huddles, or meetings
- increased absences
- abnormal outbursts
- mistakes with seemingly noncritical tasks
- dismissing awards or achievements
- lack of initiative
- physical exhaustion
- employees leaving for the day without saying goodbye

Let's be clear: a worker reporting they are burnt out *could be* self-inflicted because of poor sleeping habits, situations at home, physical conditioning, or a laundry list of other circumstances. There are, no doubt, times when an employee may be overwhelmed by various matters that are separate from the hectic work environment. And sometimes they can get conflated. If you were to ask them, they would have difficulty separating the two. But what I am offering for you to consider is burnout, knowingly or unknowingly, being leader-manager induced. Where there is smoke, there is fire. When you identify an individual feeling burnt out, be on the lookout, there are more out there.

TOMMY

Tommy was a college hire to a managerial position with a fantastic company that is experiencing remarkable growth for twenty straight years. Tommy was a fun-loving, competitive spirit. He enjoyed the back-and-forth banter with his team and had this wonderful laugh that caused you to laugh too. Tommy would make sure everyone showed to the end-of-week breakfast spot. Initially, you could always count on Tommy for a good joke or two, but over time you saw it less and less. I cannot put a finger on the trigger point, but suddenly Tommy began taking things very seriously. Tommy was excited about being hired on, and because of his personality he dove straight in at one hundred miles per hour. During the first weeks of his onboarding, Tommy sensed the pace was extremely fast, and he convinced himself that he had to concede to the tempo in order to be taken seriously. Over the next several weeks, Tommy began reporting to work two hours prior to his shift and even staying late by an hour or two—fourteen hours a day! Finally, during a midshift manager's huddle, a senior manager barked at Tommy about a topic that he updates on but only had a surface-level understanding. Tommy took the admonishment super hard. That, along with his poor rest cycle, was taking a toll on him. Although there are other contributing factors, Tommy was suffering from *self-inflicted* burnout. After a while, you could figure out that he struggled with confidence is some areas. He would spend quite a bit of time being perfectly prepared for any encounter with the senior managers. Although that was noble, it took time away from his responsibilities on the floor. This certainly caused us to keep an eye on him. Tommy was saying he was good to go. He still joked around, smiled, and moved quickly through the building. But little did the undiscerning know, Tommy was worn out. In an effort to remain in the insistent company's good graces, Tommy would take chances so it would look like he was performing at peak level. But even when being warned by his peers, he would continue the risk-taking. Tommy was trying to show he was a top talent, but the burnout forced him to take risks. You can see how the burnout was working against his energy level and weighed on his mental resilience. We all knew Tommy was all in and dedicated to the company; there was no doubt about that.

There are a percentage of Tommys out there who are self-destructing right under your noses. While at the same time Tommy is showing you his excitement for the job to prove that he belongs. He, like others, will shift to another gear—a phenomena that is seen in athletes and fervent competitors that often take them to a dangerous place of exhaustion just to score. Not coincidently, Tommy is a high-performing college athlete. People like him are internally falling apart and running out of steam. Every bit of their body language communicates they are fully engaged. But what you cannot sense are the headaches, high blood pressure, and insomnia, even though they are exhausted. In fast-paced companies that are physically demanding, all of this can be missed until, of course, Tommy's body gives in. And like all other situations in which leaders report not having time for employee engagement, I can guarantee you time will be found when Tommy no shows to work, hurts himself, or has a medical emergency. That is why owning the environment is crucial, including paying attention to the health of your employees. And at some point, you have to compel Tommy to take a knee.

Sometimes we use idioms like, "Suck it up!" "Get over it!" or "Figure it out!" Of course, that only lends to increased burnout. And not only do your people continue to feel this way, now they believe it is being orchestrated by *your* carelessness. So leaders have to look at burnout as an unhealthy condition. And like any illness, burnout can be contagious and will require some form of intervention—contagious because if one sees another finding success, they duplicate their activity, unknowing that their standard-bearer is worn out. Burnout may rest dormant, but it will lay in wait only for a catalyst, or any thoughtless person of authority, to activate it. And no doubt about it, dealing with your employees coarsely, tasking them recklessly, or addressing them without a modicum of empathy will surely inflame any process issues that actually are their chief complaint.

Indeed, there is a syndrome that lingers from burnout. It is just a matter of time before one physically breaks down. As a leader, you have an opportunity to analyze faces, discern nonverbals, and actively listen for quiet outbursts of burnout. Even though burnout is an individual's condition to reckon with, leaders hold increasing responsibility for the environment they muster. You have to keep an eye open for low energy, poor management of stress, and distancing from coworkers. But especially, look out for abnormal cynicism coming from your normally positive workers. The blind spot for leaders is when their people take on or continue to accept the responsibilities for added tasks. Because they do, you get the impression they are mentally and physically up for the tasks. There is a vicious cycle created here. The worker is unconsciously taking on tasks because they have a perceived expectation gap or because they rather do it themselves than let someone else *screw it up*. Now the worker is taking on more tasks without understanding the balance needed. It is not until they have an opportunity for clarity that they see there is not enough time or energy for more.

Psychologists see burnout as a state of physical, mental, and emotional fatigue caused by disproportionate balance. Burnout overwhelms and drains individuals. It denies you the process of reenergizing making certain you cannot meet the constant demands. Even when you try to shake it off, burnout continues to sap physical energy, which affects you mentally. And because it takes over, it spills over into your personal life, creating a cyclical effect and increasing the intensity because there are no periods of relief. It is guaranteed that those suffering from burnout are experiencing health conditions, easily contracting colds or flus.

Once you have realized that burnout is affecting your organization, you as the leader or manager ought to reevaluate the strategies that are in place. Value-stream map your team's lines of effort. Answer the question, "Are the daily tasks we are performing aligned with our objectives?" And even better, "Are we doing anything that doesn't add value to our bottom line?" It is best to have one or more of your skilled employees involved in this process because groupthink will inherently prevail in this phase. Once you have reoriented the strategy, share your new way ahead—describe what you have eliminated and what you have added. Be open to critique, but ask the team to see the new process through with a determined date to reevaluate it.

Let's talk about how this happens. It is simple. Leaders are sometimes careless when dealing out the tasks, overloading too much on one or all their plates, having crazed expectations, or getting away from their core mission. It often occurs when "bright ideas" begin to take over. I can guarantee you this carelessness is not because leaders are not concerned about their people—at least, not always. It is the juggling of too many priorities that causes one to shift a responsibility or task to another in an effort to lighten the load. Alternatively, when leaders believe that they have found a solution to an ailing problem, they insert the fix, which is undoubtedly to become an added task for themselves or delegated to a subordinate to share the load. But the bottom line, not enough thought was given to the impact on the employees. In fast paced organizations, this is certain to happened because of the fire-and-forget nature of the business. Managers are reaching for results and they are grasping at anything to obtain them even if it increases their own load. This is popularly known as mission creep.

Mission creep is one of things that *just happens*. It is similar to overloading; I would bet none of it is done purposely . No leaders want to *intentionally* make their team miserable. But I suspect one urgent priority prevailed over another and decisions were made in a vacuum without analyzing the people-impact. When you finally get a chance to take inventory of the workload, it becomes clear there is more work than hours and more energy than what can be reasonably expected out of a human. Even when new processes are introduced in an effort to streamline tasks, they are inevitably *added* tasks without subtracting the old. For a burnt-out worker, this is the "damnedest" part.

What do you do about it?

1. Call time-out. Stop and lighten the load completely.
2. Identify the problem. What circumstances take them over the edge?
3. Repair the damage. Address leader-induced concerns. Streamline work.
4. Implement a fix. Make a time-managed plan.
5. Follow up.

As a leader, you have to own this condition in yourself and others. This condition naturally winds up being wrongfully placed on the worker when this is a leadership issue. You know, there is nothing wrong with acknowledging you have pushed your people too hard. That kind of apology will go a long way to stopping the bleeding. You can identify exactly the one, two, or three tasks that are exasperating the condition. Then determine how to repair the damage to get them back to health. You will have to implement a long-term fix that levels out the demands at work. Then naturally follow through and follow up. Trust me with this: burnout can be relieved and heals quickly. It just takes a consistent positive effort and a bit of trust on your part. If you have read my blogs, I frequently talk about emotional intelligence because raising your EQ, specifically when it comes to burnout, will remove the barriers to your healthy team's optimal performance.

Managing burnout means that you continually are engaged with your people and specifically with your direct reports. You will have to be conscious of the symptoms and how they manifest. Even when things are going well, burnout can still be brewing under the surface. That is the formidable part about it. Of course, when you can identify the symptoms, you can apply the therapy, because burnout weighs on your resilience. It could be a person's mental resilience, social resilience, physical resilience, or even spiritual resilience. When that happens, the puzzle of resilience takes shape. What I mean is, it is like when you put a puzzle together. Many begin with its borders, which are often irrelevant, where you only see the sky, an ocean, or flowers. Regardless, you cannot ever make out what the puzzle's central theme is about, but you do get to frame it. It is not until you get to build out the puzzle does it reveal the project's subject. If you understand my parallel, to identify burnout you have to get a hold of more revealing puzzle pieces to expose the compromises to their resilience's protective covering. That is done by being more intrusive, using open communication, and acting with care.

Good luck—they are counting on you.

CHAPTER 12

THE LEADER'S BROKEN THERMOSTAT

LET US START THIS CHAPTER with a few questions.

What is the temperature in your organization? I do not mean how hot or cold it is. I mean, what is the temperature setting of the organization's health, its morale, or its satisfaction? When was the last time you even checked it? Have you *ever* checked it? And what temperature would you suppose it be to indicate that your team is of good health, or worse, at risk? When a human is at risk, it manifests a temperature above and below the median range of ninety-seven to ninety-nine degrees. That is just three degrees that you have to be keenly aware of to alert you that your team's welfare is functioning optimally or poorly. And like humans, what are the signs that prompt you to take its temperature? If you had just this slim of margin to determine that you are losing your team, would you be aware? Who would you check with? Where in your organization or on your team would you check? I know this is weird, but where would you even place a thermometer to gauge its health? These are all the questions you have to ask yourself as the thermometer and thermostat of the organization or team.

- Thermometer: instrument that measures
- Thermostat: component that senses the temperature of a physical system and performs actions so the system's temperature is maintained near a desired set point

As their *thermometer*, effective leaders are constantly probing the organization's health. The signs are not entirely obvious, so you will have to be paying attention to when things are not going well. When you see the team smiling, speaking positively to one another, sharing ideas, and cheering one another on, you can bet that its general health is not at risk, but that is not an absolute. And just the opposite is true. When your team stops talking to its leader, or when it stops talking at all, you have to know it is at risk. In my opinion, I would look at the trust account to gauge the risk. Well-run and healthy organizations operate on trust where its leader has built equity. Poorly run and unhealthy organizations operate on authority and strict adherence to a detailed policy where judgment, gray areas, and trust do not subsist. As its thermometer, you can bet you will hover consistently at a critical level and remain at risk while the account is low.

> YOU WILL KNOW THAT YOU'VE LOST YOUR TEAM WHEN THEY DON'T TRUST WHAT THERMOSTAT SAYS.

As the team's *thermostat*, you should be able to sense the adjustments you can *and should* make to influence your team's optimal performance. I have probably been beyond the acceptable limit of analogies for one chapter with regards to human health, but this *normal* range is a very slim margin, and you can easily teeter from the critical point of infection to the point of good health. As a result, your leadership antennae must be fully extended to hear, see, and sense good and bad conditions. Like with the thermometer, it begins with winning the campaign of trust followed by raising your EQ as you interact with your people. Search internally. Are you provoking the risk? How are you reacting to issues? Are you effective at nudging them back into that normal range? Because by acting impulsively, you will effectually lose the organization, as the team will stop coming to you. Like a thermostat, your people will have to have confidence that you can and automatically will make the adjustments to relieve the organization of its stress or poor health. And like any thermostat, you acknowledge the upper and lower boundaries and apply the appropriate care that brings the temperature within limits. Are *you* the catalyst for motivating the team? If not you, then who? Are there internal fires or bickering on your team? What adjustments are you making or are you ignoring them? Does your team look to *you* to make the adjustments? I would offer that you will know you have lost your team when they do not trust what the thermostat says.

THE UNION REP

-----Original Message-----
From: Timeforchangeintwobwoperationsnow
[mailto: timeforchangeintwobwoperationsnow@yahoo.com]
Sent: Friday, December 23, 2011 2:32 PM

To: Bravo, Christopher H

CC: Truncated x16

Subject: Operations Technicians are FED UP with Back-office!!!

This letter in intended for Mr. Chris Bravo, Ms. Tammy Mills and Mrs. Stacy Bean.

MESSAGE FOLLOWS:

The breeding of the toxic culture in the Operations Section has gotten to a point where it needs to stop. The obvious favoritism, double standards, lack of leadership and unfair practices is coming to a bubble and needs to be addressed. On many occasions, technicians have voiced their opinions only to have them ignored, avoided, and disregarded. The purpose of the letter is not to threaten, but to inspire change; to make this Operations Section an enjoyable place to work, instead of coming to work hearing the latest news about how back-office is screwing the operations desk workers. Let's start off with back-office needs to pull their own weight.

For example, every time when Ms. Mills and Mrs. Bean "do" work their mandatory minimum of two shifts a month (if they decide to work the 2 days), they schedule themselves with two certified technicians so that they can leave and float around as they please and still meet the requirement of having two certified technicians on shift at all times. The issue I have with this is that they would rather take the off day of an extra tech so that they can come and go as they please than to pull their weight like everyone else. To add to this atrocious situation, all of their passwords to all the daily programs are expired and they show no initiative to have them updated. On numerous occasions, Ms. Mills or Mrs. Bean have shown up for shift and would immediately state something to the liking of "All of my passwords are expired" in a condescending manner, insinuating that they will not be doing any work. I've even witnessed them, during exercise time, go back through and "pencil whip" the events log to show that they have in fact have worked their 2 mandatory shifts a month when they really didn't. Is that the way a Senior Managers should act? Is it ok for Senior Managers to show up for shift without everything they need to be able do the mission? This is unfair no matter how you look at it. Rank does have its privileges, but rank should not be used for personal gain. It would be a lot better in the Operations Section if the back-office worked more operations desk hours.

There is no excuse for back-office not to pull more operations desk shifts, giving the regular operations desk workers more time off with their families. They look at working the operations desk as beneath them. It's pointless for operations desk workers to be scheduled for four consecutive 12-hour night/day shifts at a time, while the back-office enjoys working Monday through Friday for 6-8 hours, with lunch, fitness time, and weekends off. The Operations Section is very top heavy, (more back-office personnel assigned, than operations desk workers), and due to the moronic management of the leadership, operations desk workers are often working long hours with little sleep and no time for fitness. It's even worse working consecutive 12-hour night shifts; your sleep cycle is off, you wake up with migraines, and on many occasions, people have mentioned dozing off at the wheel on the drive home after consecutive 12-hour night shifts. Why can't we work 8-hour shifts like the back-office enjoys? Every time it is asked, they scream "Manning" when that is not the case because it has been done before. The real reason is that if technicians do go to permanent 8's, the back-office will have to pick up slack, and that's a "no-no." We need someone to come in and properly arrange the manning and work schedule because the present leadership lack the necessary aptitude to do so. Another common practice of back-office is that they give themselves comp days. For example, the operations desk manager creates the schedule, and forwards it to the Training Office for them to insert training days. After that, it goes to the Superintendent for final approval. What usually happens after that process is Mrs. Bean runs to Ms. Mills and complains about how the schedule is made. Mills then changes the schedule so that she will work her mandatory 2 shifts on the operations desk (when she *does* work them) on a Wednesday and a Thursday. What is the significance of that? Well, she will work operations desk on those two days and then give herself a comp day on Friday and then "Bam!", three-day weekend. Their justification for giving themselves comp days is because they worked a 12-hour shift. Big deal! What about the technicians that work 12-hour shifts all the time on the operations desk? I guess we don't deserve it.

Things are seriously getting sloppy. For example, according to the Operations Section Regulations, next month's schedule is supposed to be completed and posted no later than the 15th of the previous month to give operations desk workers time to schedule various appointments. Guess when December's schedule came out, December 2nd! Never mind if the parents on the operations desk have to schedule childcare, never mind if someone was planning on scheduling a doctor's appointment. That is not a concern to back-office supervision. Why does the schedule change so often? Seems like every month, the schedule is changed at least three times. I could understand if the change was to accommodate the mission, but that is not the case. The patterns of the schedule change indicate that it is the personal wishes of the back-office that drives the many schedule changes. For example, a back-office individual might be working a set of shifts and then all of a sudden, they are off and an operations desk worker, which was previously off, is now working with little to no notice. Then you find out that the reason for the schedule change was so that someone from the back-office wanted to go out of town on a personal trip. If someone had a death in the family, I would be more than willing to take their shift, but this is ridiculous. This is proof that all opportunities are in the back-office.

First of all, you will not get a back-office position unless you are going to be a "Team Player." What I mean by "Team Player" is that they won't let you back there unless you feel comfortable about all the screwing back-office does to the operations desk; you must be willing to conform to the way of life in the back-office. All awards, opportunities, and recognition are given to back-office personnel. Even though the technicians are the reason that Operations Section passes its inspections, we still receive no recognition. During exercise time, back-office asks the technicians to help them get their programs ready to be inspected. Afterwards, they take all the credit and the awards, but the operations desk worker that helped them are left out in the cold. The only thing that is given to the technicians is more hours and hard work. I don't mind working long hours for the mission if there is a light at the end of the tunnel, but there is none. There is no hope in the Operations Section that things will get better as long as Ms. Mills, Mrs. Bean, Mr. Bravo are here. Not to mention, our Tier 1 and Tier 2 technicians, who are out on assignment, are also a part of this systematic oppression. If we don't fix it now, then it will get worse once those two get back to Headquarters. It has been brought to my attention that after only 3-4 months in the Security Manager position, Mr. Briggs is getting put up for an out of cycle promotion. There is no way that he has done enough in that time frame to deserve a stripe to be given to him. There are so many other technicians that perform head and shoulders over this peon but because he is in the back-office, the management is going to present Mr. Briggs to the General Manger as "The Guy." On many occasions myself and other technicians have witnessed his Manager competence of the job. Plenty of times, Mr. Briggs would be called early in the morning because of a system failure, but he will ask you to call someone else because either he would have people at his house or because he is in Texas working at his construction job where he gets paid under the table. Security forms would be Managers correctly filled out and the alternate would have to fix his issue, but does Mr. Briggs thank the people who have his back? No. He goes to Ms. Mills and takes all the credit. This guy is a tool. Don't try to voice concern about Mr. Briggs' behavior either, because he is their "Golden Boy." If you do, you will get reprised, the kind you cannot prove in the form of getting looked over for traveling teams, assignments, etc. He cannot do any wrong, if he does, then back-office will ignore the error and go about business as usual. He gets what he wants, comes and goes as he pleases. Back-office takes care of Back-office. He is protected. Let a Tech make an error on security documents, Mr. Briggs will rat you out to the back-office and throw you under the bus just to make himself look good. It's a dog-eat-dog world in here. If the Leadership would ask the technicians how they are doing every once in a while, most of these issues would not exist. Which brings me to my next topic; Leadership has no interest in communicating or getting to know their personnel.

Every Operations Section that I have been to, the Director and the Superintendent will bring you in and have a talk with you. They would ask about your plans during your time in the Air Force, ask about your family, are you going to school etc. That has yet to happen here. They show no initiative to get to know the people who work for them. The initial feedback session is also an opportunity for the Director/Superintendent to set standards, to let you know how to be successful. If they took a little more time in getting to know their troops, it would allow them to be able to fill positions based on individuals' strength/weaknesses. It also creates good environment and lets us know that we are appreciated. They have no interest in doing that. I wish that my Director and Superintendent were leaders that I could model myself after. The only thing they did show us is what not to do. The Technicians see all the unjust activities going on and you would be a fool to think that we do not.

Ms. Mills, you need to step up and be a leader for once in your life and stop running, ducking, and hiding from responsibility. Why are you giving the Reservists such a hard time? The childish feuding with them needs to stop. You are a Senior Manager, and you should act like it instead of disgracing the rank. Mrs. Bean, you are the ring-leader. Ms. Mills and Mr. Bravo don't know any better about how to run the Operations Section, but you do. Not only do you know how Operations Section works, you know how to work it in your favor. It is you that are influencing the decisions that are made. You do this all from the training manager's position, by the way, have you even taken the Training Managers Course? I know that you haven't because your training program sucks. Maybe if you dedicated as much time to your program and making sure that new Technicians are properly trained as you do screwing the operations desk and fulfilling your own desires, maybe this will be a better place. Also, where were you when we were moving into the New Operations Section? Why did you think you should take leave during the days of the move while everyone else (excluding Mr. Bravo and Ms. Mills) was busting their ass?

Now to you Mr. Bravo. You are the worst of them all because you are the highest-ranking individual in the Operations Section, and see all of this going on, but you choose to do nothing about it. Maybe if you were not out of the office running 5ks all the time you would know what is going on right under your nose. Maybe Ms. Mills is purposely keeping you in the dark, telling you everything is fine when it's not. There is no excuse that you don't know about the low morale, the toxic culture and the oppression that is going on in the Operations Section. How about you grow a pair, stand up, take action, and do something! For me to have to talk to you in this anonymous manner shows two things; that the situation in Operations Section has reached dangerous levels and that the fear of reprisal is real. It's your responsibility. I would like to address these matters in the training meeting, where it should be, but you, Ms. Mills and Mrs. Bean, are never in attendance. Do you, Ms. Mills and Mrs. Bean even take your EA test like you should? Think you can pass a 50 question EA certification test?

It seems as though that the back-office leadership is purposely making life harder for the operations desk workers because of all the complaints we voiced. Reason being is that they are never able to justify the things that they do. They just want us to shut up and color and if we have an issue and let them know about it, life will get harder for the operations desk workers. I want to believe that you are just oblivious to what's going on around here but I don't think you are that stupid. You cannot be that clueless. Back-office needs to have a sit down with the Technicians and iron these things out like adults, it will benefit us all. Everyone in the Operations Section has been cc'd this same message. Are you going to address these issues or continue to avoid them? We all need to have a sit down and iron out all of this together and like adults. Failing to do so will be proof to all the Regional Operations

Section technicians that you truly don't care about our concerns and refuse to do anything to correct them. Let's handle this in-house and make some changes. I want to see results and less talk. The ball is now in your court!

Best believe if you are not probing the temperature in your organization or on your team, there is certainly someone who is taking note of the temperature. And if you are not making the adjustments to calm the herd or simply make things right, there is someone on your team filling that role. The union rep is my figurative undrafted, influential ringleader who has bitten the apple and has offered a succulent bite to all other employees so they can see the world as they do—but often with less clarity. If you fail to act, trust me, they are talking about it. And the union rep is getting them all amped up. It is probably important to understand the modus operandi of a union rep. If you are trying to identify who your union rep is, the person is particularly popular. They do not necessarily have to have a great personality; they just tend to be engaged with people around them. They often have tenure and know the ropes about how administration or operations decision-making flows. They share personal information or gossip about people as they get it. Sometimes the union rep is trusted by a manager and unknowingly fed internal business-level information that is not ready for the full organization's consumption. When the union rep reveals the information, they are fueled by being the first to break it. And not only that, but they are also even more encouraged when asked to find more, making them incredibly dangerous to predecisional initiatives, processes, policy, or decisions. Because they do not hold the complete picture to how things are being run, they will spin it to their benefit or to how they see it. And certainly, if the content is juicy, they cannot wait to get it out. When the union rep breaks the information, they will never reveal their source because they must maintain their role. But what makes the union rep more powerful? They bring matters about their peers to the management team and warn them of impending revolts if they go down a certain path. Because of that, managers appreciate their value and sometimes go to them when they are about to make an abnormal business decision that will impact the team. It is then when the union rep position is formalized and fully established.

Like I said, it is easy to determine when your organization is in good health. The signs are clearly there. But if you are paying attention, the signs are just as clear when it is in poor health. Regardless of the team's size, an effective leader is constantly probing for health and welfare across the organization. They are judging morale, productivity, quality of work, safety, and barriers to achieving goals. Maintaining the three-degree temperature range is the make or break. The upper and lower limits are both points of danger. Too low signals disengagement and indifference. Too high indicates potential burnout or stress. As you go through your day-to-day grind of material production, medical care, administrative support, or logistics operations, you will have to constantly make adjustments to preserve the organization's productive health. As a skilled leader, employee engagement is the single probe that is used to determine the dialing up or down. And trust is the mechanism to steady its overall health. The two go hand in hand. In real life, a thermostat is actually a primal mechanism to read the temperature of its environment. But it still plays such an important role in changing the atmosphere. The problem is that a faulty thermostat poorly reads and inadequately relieves. Beware of the broken thermostat.

Does your team trust *you* as its thermostat?

CHAPTER 13

VERBAL COMMUNICATION:
A LESSON FROM THE NATIVES

THE WORD *HOW* IS A pop culture Anglicization of the Lakota word *hau*—a Lakota-language greeting by men *to men*. The term *hau* is often found in stereotypical and outdated depictions of Native Americans made by *non*-Natives in some Hollywood movies and various novels. But guess what—there is no such universal Indian greeting. The original inhabitants of North America spoke some five hundred different languages, and this colloquialism is not one of them. This one in particular was not standardized for all Natives, just like any other arbitrary word would not be homogenous for all inhabitants of the entire African continent. But in this context, the idiom surely deescalates things from a greeting's perspective, especially upon a first or chance encounter. Because as one closes in physical proximity, the other party is rapidly resolving if their convergence will be hostile or friendly. So how do you communicate to them that you do not want to hurt them? If you go along with the Native saying, you just say, "Hello." And you tell them you do not want to hurt them—I know, funny. If you play along, the classic way to do this, of course, is with the old standby of "Hau, I come in peace" to indicate your intentions.

So here we are. When I wrote this, we were sixteen weeks into a global pandemic brought on by the coronavirus. We have been forced to wear facial coverings while in public to protect one another from the scourge of the virus. But to prevent the US economy from its tailspin, we had to find our way back to our daily grind to prevent an almost predictable recession, loss of small businesses, and a scare of rampant unemployment. As we retreated back to our cubicles, corner offices, warehouses, or battle stations, our responsibility to lead and influence optimal performance had not lifted. But the context and social distances have certainly complicated it. I am certain you will agree that having two-thirds of your face covered is a barrier to trust and effective communication. So we will have to take the example from the fictional American Indian greeting and explicitly state our intentions or maybe a "My Name is …" sticker to warn of your intentions in an effort to lower their defenses as you hail your employees.

We have all learned in a basic leadership training that nonverbals make up 93 percent of communication. But what if 75 percent of that nonverbal communication is worn on your face? And what if 66 percent of that is completely covered? Your facial expressions convey happiness, confusion, sadness, surprise, anger, and excitement. But under a covering, those expressions could all be missed. So as a leader, communicating *verbally* and beginning with a "Hau, I come in peace," or whatever clear verbal cues you would use, it must bridge the context of the encounter. This can no longer be taken for granted or be assumed.

Your verbal communication is *now* being adjudicated. And my point is, more than ever, you must clearly communicate what you have allowed your facial expressions to command. Not only subject-verb agreement but the who, what, and why to maintain influence in this new environment. You cannot leave it up for debate. Taking this a step further, the volume, cadence, and frequency of your voice will come into play even more, given it is 44 percent of your verbal communication. Think of the emotional intelligence indicator of self-awareness. Ask yourself, "How do they see me and understand me under these conditions?"

But even another step further, your ability to read the volume, cadence, and frequency of your employees and understand *their* circumstances are even more intricate. Because beforehand you were able to see the distress or elation in their eyes or on your workers' faces, but now you have been cheated of that.

Eyes *could* indicate discomfort, desire, or distress. Staring *could* convey interest, but also a threat. Rapid blinking *could* indicate anxiety, and slow blinking *could* convey strategy. See how complicated this is? When you can simply say, "Hau, I come in peace." I have done some reading about Muslim women who wear or have worn the burqa, a traditional full-face covering of the more fundamental practitioners of Islam. No matter what your position is on this demographic of people being obliged to wear a covering, Muslim women have learned to exercise the nonverbal use of their eyes by "eyebrow flashing" to reveal that they acknowledge your presence. They have learned the temporary welling of bags underneath their eyes can communicate they are gleefully smiling. They basically wanted to show that having their faces covered was not going to be barrier to communication. And just because they are covered does not mean that they are not able to communicate verbally. Even under the covering, *A salamu alaykum*, translated to "Peace unto you," is a very close translation to the American Indian greeting of "Hau, I come in peace."

Communication is not conversation. Communication travels in one direction from sender to the receiver. Conversation is two-way. So, if we want to raise the bar with our communication in this face-covered, ambiguous environment, you will have to speak in manner that does not leave the topic up to interpretation with using nonthreatening discourse and especially when conveying problems. But when you are attempting to present a problem, this can get complex unless you are inviting a conversation. The invitation permits the other to actively participate, which is a mandate to resolving tough problems. The problem is that some leaders try to solve interpersonal problems and do it without conversation. Resolving issues have to be intentional. And as the leader, you should be thinking with the end in mind. Answering also how do you want the receiver to *feel* in addition to what goal you want them to achieve. By navigating through the communication and conversation process, it will assure you get a better outcome. It is IDEAL. Here is some timely advice: After investigating the issue and knowing all that can be known about it, describe the problem to the receiver without *ever* saying always or never. *Always* and *never* generalize and distract the conversation from what it was intended to address. By rejecting these edicts, you block out tangential matters, even if they relate, and focus on the problem in front of you.

Next, it is particularly important to introduce the effective impact by explaining how the issue made you personally feel. The thought of an emotional connection has a way of translating internally. "Your comments hurt, and I had difficult time focusing on job the rest of the day." Explaining also how their actions impacted the group or the operation creates a cooperative reaction. Now you can begin the conversation. Asking open-ended questions that steers the receiver to participate and increase your understanding is ultimately what you are trying to achieve. You never want to get out in front of an answer by being accusatory only to find out that you are confronting the wrong person or your facts are incorrect. Asking a question brings clarity to the situation and focuses on the root cause, even if they are in the wrong. Like I said, without a conversation, you can never reach a healthy resolution.

Finally, after coming to the determination that their actions hurt themselves or the team, you should collaborate with the receiver to list possible outcomes that prevent future gaffes. It will not be beneath you to agree on parts. Meaning, the leader has a part in the outcome, and the employee has a part in the outcome. Whether it be communication or performance, either way, agreeing on parts forces all parties to be accountable.

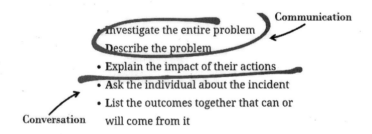

Communication

- Investigate the entire problem
- Describe the problem
- Explain the impact of their actions
- Ask the individual about the incident
- List the outcomes together that can or will come from it

Conversation

Let me take this one step further. Carefully navigating through the IDEAL process means the outcome matters. The relationship matters too. So, if you value the relationship, communicate in a way that creates positive outcomes regardless of the circumstances. Just remember, *they picked you* to share their grievance. *They came to you* to share their good news. There were a number of managers who they weaved around and between to get to you, just to share good or bad news with precisely the right person who they valued, trusted, and respected. What I am saying is, you must understand that if you are not actively building the relationship you are errantly destructing it. Not taking responsibility for the communication directly speaks to your effectual relationship. In fact, your people are weighing your relationship regularly by the words that you use and the affirmations that you sidestep. Active-constructive communication is intentional and considers the relationship. Here is an opportunity to draw from your strengths and communicate back in a way that puts them at ease, makes them more empowered, assures them solidarity in your relationship, or gives them confidence. It is a trust account deposit. You, as the leader, just have to show up and be responsive and in the moment.

Ultimately, our people *still* need to be led in these pandemic conditions. The goals and objectives of our occupations still have to be met. You have to maintain trust while your communication is in the cast of a facial covering. But how you communicate in this volatile and complex environment will determine your effectiveness as a leader, the strength of your organization, and the ability to raise morale under tough circumstances. The reality of two-thirds of your nonverbal facial communication being covered does not let you off the hook. It is about being intentional and thinking about outcomes. So use plain text. Make sure your emotions and words match. Know that sarcasm could fall flat or cut like a knife. Sincerity goes a long way at forging relationships and establishing connections. If you are *not* mad, tell your face. If you are happy, you may need to tell your face. But bottom line, you must verbally communicate and know that word choice in this new landscape matters.

Eventually, we will unmask ourselves from this pandemic and return to using our natural nonverbals to our traditional communication. Even when we do, we will have *to again* be aware of what our expressions convey. But if we continue be clear in our communication by speaking with candor and navigating through the IDEAL problem-solving method, we will disarm our people from feeling threatened or defensive while attaining the outcomes that we were set to achieve. Let this experience of having our nonverbals concealed improve our effective communication and listening skills.

Until we *actually* see each other again: "Hau, I come in peace."

CHAPTER 14

LEADING WITH THE PLAGUE OF UNCONSCIOUS BIAS

I WILL BE A LITTLE stereotypical here. What image or thought formulates in your mind if I were to say *Tyrone*? How about if I said Becky? Of course, your mind took you to a place where or when you knew these two people personally or have heard of them. Then your mind led you to the references associated with their names. It also steered you to a good or bad experience that involved one or the other. And then it also made you smile, perk up, frown, or think. We all know that Tyrone is typically Black. Jokingly, we refer to Tyrone as an unknown Black male. The name was very popular for Black males from the 1950s to the 1980s. Becky is typically white. Today the connotation is a reference to a White girl in general. But whatever your experience was or is with these two, when brought to the surface, they will forever shape what you think or know about them. It will forever generate the kind of emotions that developed when the names were posed. For some, the connection with those names will dig deep and for others it will be superficial. These are just two names that were spitballed out there—just think of themes that really have meaning. On the surface, they are just names of two humans. But below the surface are thoughts and feelings that are switched on with an ignition of experience. What you do with those thoughts and feelings will reflect on your character.

At any given moment, we receive over eleven million bits of information from the world around us. Our brains can consciously process *only* fifty bits of information at one time. To avoid overload, our brains use proxies, shaped by past experiences, cultural norms, and personal beliefs, to determine which pieces of information are important. These shortcuts are called unconscious biases, and there are hundreds of them operating outside of our awareness. If we do not implement intentional tactics and mechanisms to challenge our biases individually and as a team, they can negatively affect the quality of our team decisions and relationships.

Some people look at unconscious bias as a plague. What I mean is, we look at it with such negative connotation and as a scar on one's personality. But what you should *really* know, it is entirely natural. And it is not about ridding yourself of unconscious bias. It is about acknowledging it. Acknowledge there are blind spots in your mind's eye, its understanding, and its perspective. Because when you do recognize it, you are free to lead and are open to diverse viewpoints. But when you do not, your responsibility to guide and develop your people will inevitably be undermined. And ultimately, if your unconscious bias takes over without acknowledging it, it will ruin trust from the very start. As you know, trust is the framework to leadership, and there cannot be any obstacles that stand between your employees and trust. Here are some biases to prime your thinking:

- women with tattoos
- Black males
- LGBTQ people
- tall people
- blonde women

- heavyset people
- older people
- white men with beards
- poor people

- Asians
- homeless people

Like any good plague, most leaders will not be able to recognize when *or if* their unconscious bias has been activated. It will take a high-level of self-awareness and mindfulness to find its entry point. But unacknowledged biases, like a plague, infect your leadership output by stunting personal growth. Take a minute and ask yourself what is your first thought when it comes to each of the individual primers above? Either way, positive or negative, I recommend that you analyze the primers that you can acknowledge with root causal techniques (like the five whys) until you've reached the genesis of your thought pattern. Secondly, you could *and should* take it a step further and enrich your understanding by sitting and talking to the people you lead and open the dialogue to refine your conclusions.

WHY DOES UNCONSCIOUS BIAS MATTER IN LEADERSHIP?

As a leader, biases become obstructions to leadership engagement. You can easily discount incredible talent or even overlook emerging leaders when you are owned by them. It simply fogs your vision. And all it takes is for your vision to be faintly off, like an old pair of prescription eyeglass, to change your entire perspective. But more importantly, the establishment and loss of trust will reduce relationships to rubble. Problem: Morale, productivity, and teamwork are riding on those relationships. Any leader can be well intended but *still* act in biased ways. Unconscious bias is exactly that. It sits just outside your awareness that you do not know that they drive your decision-making or emotional responses. Unfortunately, the people around you are more aware of them than you are. Unconscious or implicit, they perceive your behavior points directly toward bias. That is why it is so essential to be self-aware and acknowledge them. If their perception is their truth, then leaders can easily be labeled as many positive or negative adjectives as possible. You have to know them before being *exposed* by them. If you are exposed, you will be wrongfully labeled a fraud or untrustworthy. Leadership and trust are a package deal.

PERIWINKLE

I met Aaron after serving thirteen years in the Air Force. I was being assigned to a unit with a physically demanding, elite cadre of logisticians, communicators, and aircraft specialists to open airfields in the most severe locations and the most treacherous of situations. I was excited. When I arrived to the unit, I was higher ranking than the current members of the element, so I would need to get spun up quickly. The responses to the September 11 terrorist attacks were still fresh. Not only that, but this particular unit was ramping up response actions to support frontline forces to infiltrate and assault those responsible for the World Trade Center attacks. So there I was. I finally completed the administrative transfer, and my trainer was going to be Aaron. Aaron was obviously gay. In my experience, up until this point, those who identified as gay or lesbian were incredibly subtle. But not in this case. Aaron was *obviously* gay and was *my* trainer in this elite organization.

"Drop your stuff. Let's go. There's a lot to train on and not much time." Off we went to get fitted for my gear and start my training regimen. Not to mention, in the next twenty days, the team was preparing to open dirt-strip airfields in the cover of night, wearing night vision goggles. I forgot to tell you: I had recently cross trained from being a dental technician, so I had no combat or operations experience whatsoever—a minor detail. Aaron moved fast and talked fast. As he helped me get fitted for my NVGs and other equipment, I could not help but focus in on his absolutely perfectly eyebrows, perfectly starched uniform with creases like a blade, and a speech pattern that confirmed Aaron's sexual orientation and he wasn't hiding it. At the same time, I quickly discovered Aaron was an expert at what we were doing and handled everything like a pro. I would never forget my thoughts in that moment: "This guy is one of the most professional sergeants I have ever met." Aaron would go on to complete my training in half the time.

In my naivety, I do not know what I thought about those who identified as gay. All I knew, it was not ever negative, and it was not ever positive. I was ignorant about sexual orientation and rationalized it in my mind like an affliction. Even though I would never treat anyone with overt disrespect because of their orientation or any other differentiation, my mind treated them as though they were different. Because I saw them as different, they got put in a box. And every single day of my exposure to Aaron tore down those walls of what I was led to believe about an individual. Here's the thing, he wasn't different, actually, but ignorance and blind spots created differentiation.

Aaron, radio call sign "Mr. Periwinkle," and I, "Mr. Orange," went out on terrific missions together as operations controllers. Just as he had shown me the ropes about owning the airfield, he had also exposed my unconscious bias. Not only was it exposed but it was contradicted. It compelled me to drop the modifier to Aaron as a gay sergeant to Aaron the sergeant. Unconscious bias does this. You cannot quite put your finger on how you arrived at the train of thought, but the idea is dug in and part of *your* social construct. It becomes the product of your understanding of the world that forms the basis for your shared assumptions about reality. Periwinkle was easily the best talent among his peers—no modifier.

With leading a diverse workforce, you have the primary responsibility to grow and develop a team where individuals feel included and valued. Your people deserve a leader who has confronted their biases with rigor. Your *own* personal growth and development are depending on it. And as you mature, you will drop modifiers from part of your vernacular. Modifiers when it comes to biases can elevate a subject. But more likely than not, they lessen its successive person, place, or thing: a female soldier, a Black judge, a lesbian manager, a disabled worker. The connotation communicates a diminished role, which also means you lower expectations. If we agree that leadership is this amazing art of influencing optimal performance in individuals, teams, and whole organizations, you ought to address your biases in which everyone is valued, and no one is limited by an insensible understanding of reality. When you do, you can guide your entire team to unlimited performance. Here are some strategies:

1. Learn and raise your EQ, specifically in self-awareness.
2. Understand the concept of bias.
3. Discuss *and listen* with socially dissimilar accountability partners.
4. Share what you have learned with your direct reports.

The idea of associating bias with a plague could possibly be a bit excessive. I realize that. A plague is a deadly affliction that is brought on by an infectious disease. It typically is eliminated with a vaccine. My association shows that biases interrupt your mental space and assign illogical meaning to experiences or insights introduced to you by primary influences. Those meanings infect how you see the world. Until inoculated with clarity will you forever think and behave by these meanings. Some have received these insights before they have even had an opportunity to experience them for themselves. Meanings like, men will take advantage or women are subservient. Plagues can be the cause of continual trouble or distress, but it all can be alleviated by a simple acknowledgment that somewhere in your social development, you associated an A and B with X or Y. So untangle your perspectives, learn the origins, and acknowledge their existence. Because leaders have a responsibility to facilitate an environment and build strong relations where the employees feel passionate about their jobs, are committed to the organization, and put discretionary effort into their work. Then and only then will your boundaries to leadership engagement be unleashed. Being constrained by these illogical meanings prevent you from establishing that environment and inadvertently oppressing some. The plague is when your biases go on unacknowledged. The impediment is when you are oblivious of their origin. But your freedom is when they are brought into your awareness.

Before I close this chapter, I am keenly aware some people hate the idea of unconscious bias and despise the idea that it labels them. They believe it is unfair and incorrectly associates them with a theme that they are unaware of or have no control of. But that is it! That is why understanding unconscious bias reveals a new layer about you. In some cases, it can deconstruct an unfortunate conflict you may have had when you have been blamed for behavior you did not intend. Since leaders have such and impactful role in managing the environment of the workplace among a very diverse composite of people, the words you choose and behavior you exhibit will be arbitrated continually. Let's be honest, some of us have been raised to believe ideas about others that stereotype or range on the spectrum of racism, bigotry, or misogyny. Throughout your life experience, you will validate or disprove those ideas when they are addressed. As a leader, however, there is a perpetual open season on how they perceive your stance on those ideas. I hope you can change your attitude on this. There is a real opportunity to take a giant step forward in an area that is difficult to grasp. Just knowing these meanings own your attitude and behavior can improve the depth of your personal power. I am certain of it.

CHAPTER 15

REASONS FOR A LEADER'S ABSENCE: IT DOESN'T REALLY MATTER

REMEMBER WHEN ONE OF YOUR leaders unexpectedly showed up in the area you work? For some reason, it generated a physiological response. Do you remember thinking, "Wow, I haven't seen her in quite a while"? And as she weaves within your spaces, you strangely get even more frustrated. Then she hovers over the shoulder of one of your coworkers and admonishes him on how he should perform a specific task. So, of course, your immediate thought is *How dare she! She hasn't been around and definitely doesn't know the struggle we have gone through to make this task work*. Even though you have been using a work-around, it has been getting the job done and meeting all performance objectives. I am sure you have seen a similar scenario like this, right? It is this kind of scenario that I have seen and heard from so many. They are frustrated that their leaders teleport in from out of the blue only to admonish them and then escape to never being seen again until the next admonishment. Strangely, employees get even more annoyed when they even show up at all from long absences. It is because they expected them to be around and they never are, so why show up now. And to take it a step further, the leader corrects their employees on processes they have been asking for their intervention long before. These are the scenarios that employees detest. Regardless if they love or loathe their management team, there is an expectation that they are around rather than behind the glass door with a coffee mug.

In my experience, I have learned employees continually beg for the presence of their leaders. Beg? Why would they have to do that? Well, where are they anyway? Actually, does it matter? It *really* does not matter. And even if they have the very best of intentions or reasons for their absence, it *still* doesn't matter. Leaders somehow find ways to get wrapped up in the managerial aspects of the job, and they sacrifice their presence to accomplish those competing priorities. And when leaders do this, especially continually, they shift out of their "leader" role. They are no longer influencing optimal performance; they are measuring, counting, analyzing, and strategizing. Don't get me wrong: those are needed tasks. But who is the thermometer and thermostat of the organization, now? It is an informal leader—not you—and everyone is taking their orders from him or her.

Trust me: If you are absent, they know it, *and* they are talking about it. And if you were following my blogs, you would have read that I have suggested time after time to constantly terrain walk. There is nothing worse than the only time you are seen is when you are escorting guests, administering punishment, or the uncomfortable time when you are introducing a new guy, and you forget the name of an employee who you *should* know.

General Dave Goldfien, the twenty-first chief of staff of the United States Air Force, says he manages his time by using the three Ds.

- Do only the tasks that your position or authority can do.
- Delegate all other tasks to the appropriate level.
- Delete: Say no when you don't have the bandwidth.

But regardless of what methodology you use to manage your time, a leader must, must prioritize presence as the most important task. When you are present, you catch people doing great work. When you are present, you understand the resource constraints. When you are present, you get to see the neglected facilities, corners, or closets. When you are present, you see your happy and your frustrated workers. And when you are present, you get to inspire and motivate your team! You can do none of this if you are absent.

As a leader, you can "Do, delegate, or delete." Or you can simply block and protect time on your calendar to go see your people and facilities. Your position as leader is much like the thermometer (measuring) and the thermostat (adjusting). As their thermometer, you can *feel* the climate of the team and their group dynamics. It is your chance to *hear* what's the talk, the rumors, and frustrations. And it is your opportunity to *see* who your informal leaders and emerging talent are. As their thermostat, you can *change* the message or discussion and *clear up* rumors. It would be a perfect time to *insert* a proper safety step or *accept* certain levels of risk. It is your opportunity to *fix* or *adjust* priorities, processes, and people.

There is more to presence than the comfort blanket effect or coercive roving patrol. Your presence multiplies the expertise where the work is being done. It creates opportunities to get answers to questions that generally would not be asked and often dismissed because of the inconvenience of going out of their way to find the boss. The idea of an open-door policy is misleading. Although the door is physically open, the psychological barrier of actually engaging the "available" boss is too overwhelming. As a result, being among the workers is far less threatening and *appears* more approachable. And finally, your presence communicates that you actually care about how the product or service is being produced. Trust me, there are a number of shortcuts being performed that you would never approve of; but your absence grants their approval.

There is another layer I think is important to discuss. Engagement plays such a tremendous role. For large companies, workers see themselves and their future in the activity of the leaders. They make preemptive career decisions if they can see themselves in your shoes when the opportunity presents itself; therefore connecting with your employees sustains retention. And there is power in committing to five minutes with each of your people. In my experience, it could be just these five minutes that creates a connection and makes your presence welcomed.

FIVE POWERFUL MINUTES

Hi! It looks like you are working super hard right now. You mind I interrupt? *No, it's OK. Wait—I need to hit the pause button.* I see your name here, but I don't want to mess it up. How do you pronounce it? *Yeah, everyone does, and it is so easy—it's Marcelles.* Ah yes, I would have messed that up. That name has a little Latin flare to it. Where are you from? *I'm from here, Tampa.* I hear an accent though. Where are you originally from? *I'm Mexican.* I *knew* I thought I heard a Latin accent. Do you still have family there? *Yes, I have lots of aunts and uncles still there.* Do you go back from time to time? *Yes! But it's been a while.* I've been to Mexico several times to a town called Zecatecas. *Really? Yes! Not many go there. It is really country.* I know; that's how I like it. So how was it growing up in Mexico? *I loved it. I miss it sometimes.* So what brings you to the company? *Well, I needed work, but also there are a lot of opportunities here.* What opportunities are you looking for? *Well, maybe IT.* Wow, do you have experience in IT? *I went to school for it and have some certifications.* Very cool. I will ask HR if there are some opportunities coming up and let you know. *Really?* Of course. Are you happy with what you're doing now? *Well, yes.* I know, but you would rather do IT—I get it. Lo estas haciendo un buen trabajo! *You speak Spanish?* Muy muy pequeno! But I'm learning. *That's great!* I'm going to try some more, but don't laugh at me! So I'll do some research and get back with you in a few hours to tell you what I've learned about IT, okay? I owe you that, especially since this data sheet says you work so hard around here. And if there aren't any of those jobs available, maybe we can talk about some other opportunities . What do you think? *Yeah!* Don't let me forget Marcelles. I'm getting old, and it gets really busy around here. *OK.* So, let's talk soon. By the way, my name is David. Everyone calls me Satch. I'm the new manager here. *Yes, I know.* I'm sorry for not talking to you sooner, but I'm glad we did. Set the timer—I'll be back to see you. Estas bien? *Si! Gracias.* OK Chau!

That was a re-creation of my first *real* conversation with Marcelles. As you can see, this conversation is all about Marcelles and all about building a connection anywhere you can find one. There is always something you can connect with. It is your job to find it. Even if it is about food, or a book, or travel, or family—find the connection. Oftentimes, with males, sports become the go-to connection, and it is so easy to establish it. Definitely go there—it opens the windows to relationships. But the bottom line, do not fake it. If you are not a sports fan, do not act like you are. Employees are already skeptical of their leaders. So do not give them any ammunition to call you a fraud. If it was a good encounter, three more people will know about it. If it was a bad one, seven more people will know.

Another shortcoming that occurs due to a leader's absence is the "meetings of the minds" by the people who actually *do not* make the decisions. They crunch the numbers, debate the legitimacy of policies, and deliberate on who should be off work and when. When leaders are absent these grapevine discussions form and allies become united. Depending on their solidarity, the conclusions they arrive at could sometimes become the standard.

I HEARD IT THROUGH THE GRAPEVINE

There are several claimed origins of the grapevine. One heard in the song "I Heard It through the Grapevine" by Marvin Gaye, and one that stems from an excerpt from the autobiography from Booker T. Washington. In his book, he refers to a colored mail carrier overhearing the news of the war. On the mail carrier's route back, he would retell what he had overheard from the customers discussing at the post office after they were picking up their mail. Another origin of the grapevine is from the Old Grapevine Tavern. Again, in the setting of the Civil War, where soldiers hung out and got news about the progress of the war. Union spies often frequented the tavern to spread rumors or inculcate misinformation. The grapevine has not changed—only the settings. It is *still* all about the keeper or spreader of information. Information power comes and goes. The more information you have the more powerful you appear to be.

But that means leaders have to consistently be "in the know." Some leaders realize they wield this power, so they are reluctant to share so they can maintain it—I know, it is strange. But one thing I know, there is a lot being said in the grapevine—some positive and a lot negative. And there is an informal leader among them, flexing his clout through the grapevine for all that will listen. I would offer that the grapevine is, no kidding, a communication vehicle that leaders should not dismiss, but actually tap into.

In the grapevine is where creative or destructive dialogue flows like white water as evidenced by social media. Even though there is no formal control over the grapevine, there are key informal leaders. The problem with the grapevine is that messages have unrestricted flow. And even if you wanted to treat a particular message like a one-on-one letter or telephone call, in the grapevine, you have no control on its wider propagation. There is one other facet about the grapevine. It travels faster than *any* other form of communication, especially *really* good and *really* bad information. Unfortunately, the grapevine has no traceable origin nor can anyone reference it because of the rumor-like nature of this communication hub. Of course, rumors invariably get altered and this is the unfortunate aspect of this message center. As a leader, it is always good to identify its central figure. That is the person you have got to get to know. You *must* know who they are and how to use *their* powers for good. Quite honestly, the information flowing through the grapevine could be 100 percent correct. But the danger is that it could also be entirely false. Just think if leaders shared everything they knew about the changes in policy, the direction in procedures, or their intent early and often into the grapevine. You could keep rumors down and information flowing. The absence of information causes distrust and conspiracy. So why do leaders tend to hoard information? Here is an opportunity to share how you arrived at decisions on nominations for promotions, picks for awards, choices in leadership positions, or changes in processes.

> ## "MILLENNIALS ARE DETACHED FROM INSTITUTIONS AND RATHER BE NETWORKED WITH FRIENDS."
> —PEW RESEARCH, 2016

It is also your opportunity to listen to what is being said, change the narrative, or stamp out conspiracies. Quite honestly, people turn to social media when our leaders are not sharing information. And just like the song, "Oh, I heard it through the grapevine. Oh, I'm just about to lose my mind," misinformation will impact morale and the climate of the organization.

There are various designs of organizational communication. But what we are learning with this new generation is that vertical communication is simply out of touch. Vertical communication is strictly shared one step above or below. It is not intended for you to convey information above your boss, even if they are available to share it. It is not intended for you to communicate two steps down either, undercutting your direct reports from their opportunity to lead. Our newer generations want wide and dynamic communication flow where it matches the speed of information that is found in technological communication streams they use today. I dare you to gather everyone in the hallway or form a huddle in the confined space of a cubicle. You could even see how many people you could jam in a small office and unleash rumor control. While you are at it, go on social media and have the same conversation. It starts with, "Does anybody have a good rumor?" and finishes with, "Let me tell you what I know."

> ## WHY LET THE GRAPEVINE TELL THE STORY? INSTEAD OF IGNORING OR REPRESSING THE GRAPEVINE, TUNE INTO IT.

Equally important to presence, the grapevine harbors unfounded truths in the absence of its leaders. Your presence affords you the liberty to weave within the spaces. It offers you opportunities to share information and hear the grumbles. Then it grants you the freedom to admonish employees without creating animosity because you have shown your interest in the work and its workers. Absence does not. Presence is difficult because it detracts our attention from the number of administrative tasks that are guaranteed to pile up. You will be afforded a limited pass with this excuse. But when used too often, they will no longer be sympathetic of your administrative workload. How you balance your presence and these tasks will be trying at times. So delegate those tasks that do not require your fingerprints, and spend more time with your people.

To maintain an increased level of personal power means that you have noticeably assimilated among your team. You know them and they know you. Because of the invested time with them, they are eager to see you and look forward to being motivated and inspired by you. They look forward to showing you something they have learned or maybe an innovation they have discovered. They look to you to fix human resource errors or situations they have been confronted with. Only presence will give you these opportunities. From my experience, I realize that presence is a risk. When you invest in presence, other responsibilities get abandoned. Unfortunately, the one principle you cannot delegate is your presence. So, block and protect your scheduled time to regularly invest in presence. Because layered under your presence is trust, commitment, respect, and credibility. Finally, you will know that trust and connections are built when they bring you their errors or own their mistakes without you seeking them out. With absence, they will not. Because if you hear, "Wow, I haven't seen you in a while," let that be your first indication that your absence is noticed *and* felt. So stop making excuses for why you are so busy. It *really* does not matter.

CHAPTER 16

THE CHALLENGE TO IGNITE MOTIVATION

WHAT METHOD DO *YOU* USE to get the very best out of your team? I am sure you have a technique, right? I knew someone who would dress up as a superhero occasionally. He would walk around greet the members of the team to incite some enthusiasm. I knew someone who would award Wonder Woman coins to deserving high performers. I knew someone who would use a motivational shtick to instill pride, enthusiasm, and passion or PEP by speaking to the team optimistically. Then there were some who simply sat down with each member of the team to encourage them in their own unique way. There is no sure, foolproof method. But regardless, you should have an approach. I was taught long ago that the thrust behind organizational momentum is a motivated team. And since this book is about inspiring effective leadership, I must, must talk about motivation. Motivation is tricky because it can get really personal. And if you ask ten people, "What motivates you at work?" you will get ten different responses. There is a lot to that and too much for a short chapter addressing motivation. But the skinny behind it is pretty simple. Each of our primary influences of family, school, religion, and neighbors are incredibly disparate. And how they influenced or motivated you will be carried with you for a lifetime. This means leaders have to adapt their style of motivation to the uniqueness of the individual.

I would be remiss if I did not address the philosophy of "awarding trophies." There was a twenty-year period of time, in the early 2000s, in which a psychological approach was introduced for parenting and nurturing children by awarding a literal trophy or ribbon for any achievement, to include their failures. In youth sports, child and adolescent psychologists suggested removing or turning off the scoreboards to forestall children from the reality of losing a contest. And even when they lost, they were *still* awarded a participant's trophy. This approach is significant to leadership and influence because those children are now adults in the workforce and have been motivated by trophies even when they underperformed. It will be a leadership challenge to negotiate when their expectation of reward has not been met. As I stated in previous chapters, primary influences have a lifelong effect until they are re-socialized by significant emotional events. So when you do not respond to their satisfactory effort with a theoretical trophy, you may find they will be demotivated. But if you hold firm, you will begin the growth process. Here is the thing: People *know* when they actually have underperformed. They *know* when they have missed the mark. They *know* when they have behaved badly—they *know*. They even know when they have not measured up against the field. So do not give credence to an approach to award an undeserved trophy. Just think, if you had a pickup game and the captain had a choice to select yourself, Kobe Bryant, LeBron James,

Michael Jordan, and Julius Irving. You should be selected dead last, right? You *know* it. But more importantly, *they know it too*. When you give oxygen to those ideas, you hamstring your people, and you perpetuate a fraudulent idea of self-awareness.

Ultimately, morale and motivation drive performance and performance drives goal accomplishment. So, if leaders want to influence optimal performance, it is imperative to still begin with this tricky skill of motivation. It is not a one-size-fits-all skill, so it is essential that leaders *first* learn what distinctively motivates the individual or team. You cannot simply use the method or tactic that motivated you. In fact, that could possibly be destructive. But if applied *just right*, you can influence them to transcend their very own self-imposed limitations. Yes, the point where they have dialed down their vision and not allowed themselves to see beyond it. Self-limitations can be completely unintended and could be derived by the attitudes of their primary influences. The motivational spectrum spans horizontally from authoritative which is extrinsic to initiative which is intrinsic, and spans vertically from healthy, an enduring value, to unhealthy, a more fleeting value. Picture *The Hunger Games*. It is classic authoritative and unhealthy motivation. Then picture my National Football League's Philadelphia Eagles in Super Bowl LII, when MVP quarterback Nick Foles suggested a trick play called "Philly-Philly" to widen the lead—the essence of initiative and healthy motivation.

So how do you put this into practice? First, leaders must establish by employee engagement the proper igniter that motivates individuals. Here are some igniters that come to mind:

- The challenger: an igniter to cause one to compete against one's self

An example of the challenger looks like this:

- (Leader): "You have performed this task remarkably well and I'd like to see you take this one step further. Do you have any more of those creative juices to take this project to the next level? I have seen what you can do. I believe you can!"

The challenger approach is the leader extracting the *will* out of their workers for them to see it for themselves. They are showing them the possibilities are just beyond their fingertips. When they are open to see it, the light comes on and they are genuinely motivated. Just know, if you are not actively building motivation, you are explicitly obstructing it. Just think about it. Motivation is based on momentum. Any obstacle to momentum requires a reset. Think about that when you are applying your methods to ignite.

Here are other go-to igniters:

- Face-Timer: active-constructive igniter (recounting their success)
- High-Fiver: passive-constructive igniter (that is, high fives, fist bump, "good job," etc.)
- Check-Writer: passive-destructive igniter (that is, days off, pay bonus, etc.)

You can easily get caught up in the vicious cycle of comparison, which is a ruse to actual competition and inspiration. Comparison is dangerous because it is not static. You end up competing against a moving target that will force you to change when, quite honestly, you may need to build on the reserves you have. Comparison forces you to consider the similarities or lack of them to drive your motivation. An apple to apples comparison could be ridiculous, especially when your Achilles heel is an orange. That would mean being your own competition allows you to improve based on the personal milestones that *you* established and not that of others. Then the motivation is against the previous day, week, or any period's version of yourself. Just think if you were motivated and made yourself your toughest competition. You would open the eyes of self-awareness and see your faults, your strengths, your biases, and your blind spots. Then you would see what is hindering your progress or, even better, what is anchoring it. The healthiest road to motivation is deep with you, not the current and new shiny rock. To *know thy own self* is a far better generator of motivation because you develop into an improved version of you rather than an imposter from your closet and wardrobe.

CRAIG

Craig was a maintenance officer for nearly twenty-five years. He was from Louisiana. They called him the Cajun. You could underestimate Craig because of his unassuming look. He is a white guy, a little round, with a bald head and mild Cajun accent. I will never forget the day we had physical training and we were running a path that lined Pearl Harbor in Hawaii. I was a decent runner and moving along just fine, when Craig comes blasting past me. "Look out for big sexy!" he says as he whisked by. Immediately after you start talking to Craig, he will suck you right in. He is amazingly positive, has a great smile, and will keep you laughing. He had one of those personalities that people always ended up sitting or standing around his desk. Craig had great stories to tell. They always centered around food, deer hunting, or the bayou. As a leader, Craig believed in empowerment.

If he saw you had talent, he would hand over the reins and let you steer. The admirable thing about Craig was he knew his limits. If he did not know, he was confident with saying it out loud. He had an incredible amount of trust in his people and they trusted him. You could see it in their effort. When you did a good job, he was certain to tell you about it. Not only that, but he would also tell you why it mattered. Even if you fell short, Craig would appreciate your effort but reorient you to get you back on track. His people still felt encouraged, even after being admonished. Craig had another talent. He could cook—I mean, he could *really* cook. And whenever there was an opportunity, Craig would showcase his chef skills. He would say, "You can't put too much seasoning!" There was story going around about Craig cooking many years ago for his entire organization. He decided to smoke entire pigs. As usual, the pigs turned out great! Everyone had a helping or two. The next day, 167 of his coworkers *and a dog* were sick from food poisoning. Craig undercooked the pigs. He will *never* live it down. One day, I was describing Craig to a person who did maintenance. They said, "Oh yeah! I remember him from like fifteen years ago. He got everybody sick." But he also said, "We knew he would be a great leader." My experience with Craig was no different. He rallied the team together and ensured there was laser-like focus on the goals. With his positive attitude, great personality, and chef skills, everyone wanted to work for Craig. Do not get me wrong, he worked hard and put in an incredible about of overtime. And regardless of his positive demeanor, you should never cross him. But that was the thing about Craig, people *wanted* to do a good job for him. And as high up on the food chain as he was, Craig made everyone feel like they were part of the team and part of a family. He had this way of leading from his core and not from his duty title. Regardless of your experience level, you would not turn down an opportunity to work for and with Craig.

You simply cannot talk about this topic without including the Theory of Human Motivation. In 1943, Abraham Maslow concluded that an individual must have their lower-level needs of food, safety, security addressed before they can reach a point that they are propelled to another motivational level. That would mean that leaders have to cultivate a climate and relationships in which their workers *feel* secure, a *sense* of trust, and recognize their purpose to catapult themselves to their fullest potential. Simply put, people cannot be reasonably inspired when they are spinning in survival mode. Survival mode is a state of existing to eat today, live today, breathe today, and survive today. Long-term challenges are not part of their calculus nor are they motivated by big dreams and opportunities. They can see them as unrealistic and unattainable reach-goals that can only be achieved by a lottery ticket or a magic trick. But when you step up and out of survival mode, you will be genuinely motivated by love and belonging and actually see your potential and creative genius. So it is important to recognize where your people are and set reasonable goals that drive them out of survival mode. If you don't, they will ignore your planned goals and you will constantly be frustrated by their effort.

In leadership, your ability to motivate your workers for just motivation's sake and influence intrinsic motivation within them is the pinnacle of motivational leadership. Using progressive techniques that ignite them to challenge themselves is your ultimate goal. If you have to constantly pedal to keep the wheels turning, this should be your indication that you need to shift techniques. A leader who is continuously pedaling, and the wheels are not equally spinning shows you have yet to connect or have not yet ignited the level motivation that corresponds with the speed of the pedaling. For instance, motivating by writing a check when they want to be motivated by face-time or by connection will cause endless pedaling. And when you stop pedaling and the wheels come to a halt, it would mean your effort was worthwhile but not shared. This can only mean your workers are not yet internally motivated. Keep igniting; you just need one spark.

This is what I suggest to motivate an organization:

1. Be visible. Get to know the uniqueness of your workers.
2. Keep it positive. Create a forward-looking climate.
3. Empower employees. Encourage them to operate on intent.
4. Take some risks. Accept their failures.
5. Motivate. Use healthy and constructive igniters.

Why does motivation matter? We can never understate or trivialize motivation and the effects on the human condition. Motivation is life's oxygen. Without it, a human can be void of purpose, which is tremendously dangerous. When you are in a jam, it will increase your physical effort and power creative thought. If you have ever seen the movie *The Hunger Games*, you can imagine the amount of motivation you would have to have to remain alive. And not only that, think creatively to defeat obstacles in your way. While writing this book, motivation helped me tune into the muse, or one's flow, to write it in a third of my planned time. Although writers find the muse in due time, enhanced motivation tends to source the muse's wavelength effortlessly. You lose track of time and find the work to be effortless. Motivation has a way of revealing the zest of your efforts. It translates the obligations of work to the privilege of passion. And when you have a passion for what you do, it will never feel like work. You will find yourself saying, "I got to be in a leadership position," to "I get to be in a leadership position." And finally, motivation converts difficult situations from negative to positive. Regardless if it is work or fun, when you are motivated, it inspires you to face challenges head-on. For instance, before taking on a tough, undefeated opponent, motivation changes your thinking from believing it is impossible to it being viable. It reduces your nerves, makes you more alert, and makes you more instinctive. When facing a twelve-foot downhill putt to win or tie on the eighteenth hole, motivation becomes the willing vehicle to your indescribable focus and the visualization of its end result.

In our world of leadership, motivation is essential to job satisfaction, personal development, and retaining top talent. Motivation says you can do it, you want to do it, and you cannot wait to do it. This is its power cycle. To get there, leaders have to willingly accept the charge of being the motivational catalyst of the team. It is the unwritten part of your job description. It is not always "rah-rah." Sometimes it is simply highlighting the pathways to their success. Because when they are motivated, they are engaged. When they are engaged, they take ownership. When they take ownership, they innovate. When you have a culture of innovation, productivity increases, and costs are reduced, closing the incredible cycle of motivation. And finally, motivation is contagious. When there is a core of inspired elements on the team, the curiosity will draw the others to motivation's gravitational pull. This is where teammates share information, compete friendly, and become committed. Commitment is motivation's second breath. And it all begins with you!

CHAPTER 17

A LEADER'S THEME MUSIC:
ARE YOUR EMPLOYEES TUNED IN?

I HOPE WHEN THEY SEE me coming they catch me two-stepping to the beats like Bruno Mars's "24-Karat Magic" thumping in my head. And I hope that it grabs their attention. I hope they start bobbing their heads, moving their feet, or even singing along. And if they did, they may have caught a bit of *my* influence. That is right—it is *my* theme music. We all have it. Some of you even have multiple tracks. With having a pop artist like Bruno, I will certainly influence the vast majority of those around me—but not all. And I realize that, so sometimes I will switch it up and walk in the office with a song like "Kiss," by the late Prince being my trusty standby. And undeniably, if Prince cannot influence them, nothing can. Where am I going with this?

I am talking about theme music. Theme music is the repeated or elaborated pieces of music that accompanies a subject. In my metaphorical illustration, theme music is the preferred leadership approach and style that is repeatedly used to motivate and inspire their surroundings. Theme music is a product of your persona that you naturally carry along with you. It is your leadership sexy. People will gravitate to you, or not, because your theme music is a serenading and reassuring comfort of character, credibility, and courage. When leaders lead by these innate tunes of strengths, they shift employees away performing at the minimum standard, to giving a committed effort. Because employees that perform tasks just when a leader demands it, they march only to the beat of a different drummer, so to speak, rather than those who sing along because they are fully committed to the organization's strategy. This shows that acting on authority alone will only yield compliance. Commitment stems from leaders operating beyond their authority activating their personal power. There is something to say about simply being your authentic self as a leader. Your people can then align with you and feel confident in trusting you with their careers. Like with all music, there are people who will appreciate the swag that accompanies your style, and there will surely be people who will be put off by it. It's certainly not a popularity contest and I would warn against competing for acceptance. Popularity is far too transitory and you can lose everything you have gained with a single reviled decision or changing things up based on business need. The tricky part about theme music is that you may have lulled yourself into a false sense of security believing the single track you have been playing can simply be looped for any group and for any circumstance.

Too often leaders transport their theme music from previous places of employment, expecting employees to immediately respond by bobbing their heads or getting behind the new leader. But oftentimes, it does not catch on. It may even be a little irritating. Because some leaders believe their leadership style is plug and play. Motivating people is not as simple as that. This can be a little confusing for you because, after all, it worked with your previous team. You will find yourself trying to figure out what is wrong with *them* when actually it is you. In your search to understand why they are not feeling the influence, you will blame their lack of motivation on poor discipline, absence of teamwork, or personality clashes. At a minimum, leaders will have to adjust their style, if even a little bit, to address the unique needs of their new team. Because although team A loved Johnny Cash, team B loathes him. This is all part of the insightful self-awareness of a leader who comes with an increased emotional intelligence quotient.

> SELF-AWARENESS: THE ABILITY TO RECOGNIZE AND UNDERSTAND YOUR MOODS, EMOTIONS, AND DRIVES, AS WELL AS THEIR EFFECT ON OTHERS.

KALETH

Kaleth is one the coolest people you will ever meet. He had one of those personalities that was easy to connect with. He somehow tended to be the center of gravity. He had a way of building friendships. Kaleth is from Columbus, Georgia. He was a tremendous athlete in basketball and football. After prematurely leaving Wright State University, he joined the United States Air Force. After a speed bump or two, he swiftly navigated up the enlisted force career ladder. Even during his early years while partying and living it up, he was still focused on his self-development. He obtained his undergraduate degree and subsequently his MBA while working fulltime. Still the life the party, Kaleth became a respected leadership development instructor. Capitalizing on his influence, he held small group sessions to help pull his circle up by challenging young men and women to raise their leadership acumen. People flocked to Kaleth because of his credibility and courage. And you wouldn't have to be convinced it was Kaleth's infectious personality and simply being a "normal" dude that caused people to gravitate to him. If you asked him, he would say he would just be himself. Kaleth continued to excel and even began building an e-mail distribution group, before there was social media, to pass-on professional development nuggets to all that would listen. He was well on his way to being a significant player among the top tier leaders in the Air Force. There is a well-known story about Kaleth's dorm room parties. One of his admirers asked if he could be invited. Kaleth agreed. When the admirer and friend showed up, fully expecting music, drinks, girls, and cigars, Kaleth had something else in mind and had set up a private feedback session because the young man had been performing well below his potential. Even during this time, his personality from the early years never wavered, and his influential circle had grown exponentially. Wherever Kaleth was everyone wanted to be. He was the custodian of incredible understanding on how to lead by personal influence. His story got even better as he was hired to be the Chief Master Sergeant of the Air Force and the eighteenth ever to be promoted to the position in its history. Still the same guy, his following could not grow larger. Understanding the issues, he made radical changes to professional development and structural policies that were hugely popular for the force. His personal example of how to lead using only his natural strengths elevated him to become arguably the best in his position. Kaleth's influential power earned him the name the Enlisted Jesus.

Just Google it, you will see.

As a leader, you will have to realize how you motivate and influence your organization. And just because you were successful motivating one demographic of people over there, motivating another population here is guaranteed to be different. Talented leaders, like Kaleth, know that individuals and teams require a unique influential experience. It is like shifting from Bruno to Prince to get the absolute best out of them. That means you will have to be totally aware of what *your* theme music does to the organization so you can shift it on the fly. If you are serious about influencing optimal performance, you have to get a sense of what motivates him, her, or them. Then take inventory of your abilities and tune to different stations. This takes self-awareness, which is just *you*, looking in the mirror at your authentic self. You do not necessarily need to change who you are. You just have to acknowledge the effects it has on others. Are you too grumpy, too moody, too hyperactive, too giggly, too strict—you get what I am saying.

- "Know thy self."
- Be honest with yourself and others.
- Acknowledge your biases.

So about those biases. It is absolutely critical to acknowledge their existence. Biases will get in the way of your ability to connect, mentor, and lead effectively. I presented a case about biases in chapter 14, "Leading with the Plague of Unconscious Bias." By now we should all agree that they occupy a space in our character. In fact, because biases are part of your unconscious mind, it can interfere with truth. Even when facts or illustrations can be right in front of you, bias has a way of discounting those realities or altering your vision. But biases can also be explicit too. They can be known by you, and you can willfully accept them. Explicit bias plays an everyday role in life, and it is wedged in your social structure. The distinction is that these biases are completely regulated by you. Explicit biases are often activated as a protective mechanism to defend yourself from threats to you physically or your founding principles. Here is an important point that I want to address here about biases that is relevant to theme music. Many experts will compel you to dispel yourself of inherent biases and I disagree to a point unless, of course, they provoke discrimination. For instance, if you had a family member killed by a drunk driver, you have probably formed a bias about those who drink alcohol. It is not as simple as *abracadabra* to rid yourself of that implicit memory that is on autopilot. Therefore, you have to acknowledge (1) it is a bias, (2) that you walk around with it, and (3) you cannot allow it to control your decision-making. In my military experience, I have had to negotiate with my biases on occasion that unexpectedly appeared before me. And as my boss's senior advisor, I was trusted to advise on the discipline of the workforce. So, when I was presented a criminal investigatory case, sometimes you would find that the circumstances of the case trips on one of your own personal experiences that puts you in an awkward position. I clearly have a bias, and it could be unfair to the worker if I did not include the disclaimer of acknowledged bias as part of my advice. Having raised a child who had been assaulted would put me in terrible position to provide advice on an assault case. But recusing yourself from cases is not always the prudent thing to do. It might be best to acknowledge what biases you comfortably walk around with instead of trying to poorly suppress them. They are part of who you are—you have to assure yourself that they cannot become weaponized.

If you can identify the characteristics of your personal power and picture the idea of theme music, it is an even exchange. Your theme music consists of those soft skills that you use to communicate, engage, and build relationships with to motivate and inspire a team. It could be any number of your qualities. Sometimes it will be your engaging personality. Sometimes it is your credibility. But whatever it is, it ultimately needs to increase team morale, improve performance, and foster open communication. The concept of theme music is synonymous with social skill. It is your socialization or gained competence in facilitating interaction. At times, you have to try different methods to connect with hard-to-reach groups. If you have ever seen coaches in locker rooms, awkwardly dancing to today's music in an effort to motivate and inspire the team, you can bet they did a reverse discovery. And you can guarantee, it was never part of their conventional leadership approach. They learned what motivates the team and added it as part of their style—it is really that simple. Like these coaches, you cannot allow your personality type to get in the way of downloading new themes. Sometimes reclusive or introverted personalities may find difficulty in exploring new music. Extraverted personalities can switch tracks with ease. Regardless of the personality type, tuning into your team's motivation still need to be authentic, intentional, and precise. It will never hurt to simply ask what motivates them. You just might have that track in your library. Then connect by accentuating your personal powers of character, credibility, courage, and collaboration. They will carry the tune for you.

CHAPTER 18

HOW TOXIC LEADERS
GET INTO POSITIONS OF POWER

THE CANCEL CULTURE OUTING THESE PERSONS
OF RESPONSIBILITY WITH A STRAIGHT AND OPEN
HAND TO THE FACE

LET'S BE HONEST, NOT EVERY person has the best people skills but, even still, can be fantastic architects at engineering solutions that lead to mission success. To have people skills would mean you fall high on the emotional intelligence meter. You are self-aware and acknowledge your strengths and flaws. You maintain solid control of your emotions when giving and receiving bad news. You display empathy when your people need you on a different emotional wavelength. Your interaction with the team is positive and uplifting. You maintain a unique ability to motivate and inspire the various groups of people in your influential circle. But when you are lower on the meter, you will tend to be focused on the mission and miss the impact on the people. You strategize how to reach organizational goals and do absolutely whatever it takes to achieve them—even at the price of the members of the team. I imagine for some it is difficult to balance both people and production.

The challenge with leading is finding the sweet spot between people and production. And as we focus on the development of new leaders, we have to challenge their conventional wisdom when it comes to leadership and management. In this performance-driven environment, their own managers fail to identify those character flaws in these "up-and-comers," and they wind up in positions leading people without being challenged to deal with their weaknesses before being placed in charge. And quite honestly, in the transient nature of global employment, those leaders' flaws get lost in re-assignments and never get a thorough quality review, or they are assumed to "clear themselves up" on their rise to greater positions of power.

Call me naive, but I will assume 99 percent of leaders and those put into positions of power did not enter the role thinking how badly they could stir the environment into chaos, generate fear, or be as apathetic as humanly possible. I am confident people do not have a goal of being toxic. I am convinced most of us would *or should* agree on this thesis. It would assume only those who are socially inept or antisocial enter a situation like that with an agenda to be autocratic or manipulative. Those people align with that of slave owners, dictators, and tyrannical leaders. They exhibit attitudes and behaviors that are the worst among us. And unfortunately, they are behaviors that have been planted and groomed by laissez-faire leaders who have condoned their actions because it bore short-term and short-lived achievements. I would submit it is indeed in the achievement that nurtured these behaviors' approval. Do it all cost actions to pull the team across the line feed these behaviors, especially when they are rewarded. Then the reward condones and encourages "win at all cost" performances, even if rewarded unknowingly.

Other toxic words:

- virulent
- noxious
- dangerous
- destructive
- harmful

- unsafe
- malignant
- injurious
- pestilential
- pernicious

- environmentally unfriendly
- fatal
- deadly
- lethal

So how does a leader initially get to this state? From my perspective, it is a learned behavior that is actually drawn from good intentions but poorly executed by failing to consider the secondary and tertiary effects of their decision-making or statements while being the person in charge. This learned behavior is derived from values prejudiced in early ecological microsystems, such as parents, religion, neighborhood, friends, and culture—your primary influences. Those values sometimes say, "Win at all costs." They say, "People who complain are weak," or are "snowflakes." Or they might say, "If it doesn't kill you, it makes you stronger." As you know, these philosophies can drive an organization into the ground. Why? Because these values desensitize the manner in which we look at people. They become numbers, robots, or blips on computer screens rather than living, breathing people who exhibit emotions and finite energy. When leaders come to the point of seeing through their humanity, they begin to edge the toxic spectrum.

In my experience, I have seen how toxicity makes nebulous appearances. In one case, let us assume leaders would want to do a great job. They draw up a plan, make some sort of spaghetti chart, identify where the risks are, then "slap the table," and order their subordinate-leaders to execute. Toxicity makes its appearance here because the leader only saw A to B, start to finish, or open to close. But missed everything in between—the people. In another case, let us assume leaders do want a well-run organization with high morale. So again, they draw up a plan, make some sort of spaghetti chart, identify where the risks are, then "slap the table" and order their subordinate-leaders to execute. You may find toxicity makes its appearance here, as well. The leader defined the good and bad, the achievable and unrealistic, and the risky and benign. But they missed the contributing voices—the people.

THE PEOPLE DEFINE TOXIC LEADERSHIP

Assuming this 99 percent does not intend to be toxic, (1) how did one percent of them get rewarded to the corner office, and (2) how do we eradicate those flaws before they are seated there, or delay their promotion until they are proven? There is a lot to unpack here, but the organization's culture is the driver. Because if the culture says push at all cost and absorb any acceptable risk of attrition, then the company owns the losses and condones toxic leadership. But when that is not the case, leaders have to confront behavior that conflicts with organizational culture and even when the leader produces results, exceeds milestones, or raises the bar, they cannot still be placed into positions of leadership until they raise their emotional intelligence quotient. A company that gains the whole world but loses its soul will eventually reach its demise.

MITCH

Mitch was an experienced operations controller. In fact, Mitch was one of the few who was in the career field before it made its transformation. Because of his decades of knowledge in the field, and because he did incredible work as a seasoned operator early on, he was considered one of the top talents in the field. But Mitch had one of those personalities that you loved him or hated him. He made edgy comments and projected playful flirting. There were some who were turned off by it, and others thought it was entertaining. I have to admit, there were times when I was around him that I found he was amazingly hilarious. But most of the time, he would do or say things that were out of bounds. And because of that, I steered clear of him. At an annual conference, it was announced that Mitch would become the senior manager of the career field. In my very brief experience with Mitch, I could not figure out why they would select him. Maybe it was just tenure. Or maybe it was his good work that he performed in the field. Maybe he had a deep supporting cast. Maybe it was all of these things. Certainly it was not his leadership strengths. There were noticeable gaps there.

Over the next several years, Mitch made a litany of changes to the field. None of which that advanced the operation or enticed recruitment or retention. In fact, operations controllers were leaving the field faster than we could train them. And regardless of the feedback to his office, he would go in his own specific direction. If you were to elevate issues to Mitch, he would shoot them down for a variety of reasons. The problem with his team's decisions, they never considered the impacts to the people. And the people were outraged by the direction they were going. There was one thing about Mitch: he would never care about the feedback. He was kind of the "my way or the highway" type. Unfortunately, the career field continued in a tailspin. If you know anything about a tailspin, it is one of the most complicated aviation conditions a pilot can experience—it almost always ends in total loss.

When you look back, the decision makers who put Mitch in this position knew this about him and his dominant personality. They knew he trafficked on the borders of inappropriate. You can bet his many years of experience and knowledge in the field was the determining factor. And based on the feedback from the field, that certainly was not enough to rally leadership teams together, sort out the operations core functions, recruit, and most importantly retain the talent to take the field to the next level. Unfortunately, the career field remained in a tailspin even after Mitch's departure. It is not because of any of his successors' competence, but it is the utter difficulty of changing course and out of the spin. But the number one reason the organization cannot course correct the condition is because of the criteria in which they select their leaders. Experience, knowledge, and hard work were obviously the criteria for the field's selections to their top positions. If leaders evaluated Mitch's leadership portfolio and talent level, *maybe* they would have passed on him. Mitch's impact on the career field will be long lasting, and that is the danger in using the wrong criteria.

In fairness to Mitch, I do not believe for one minute that Mitch purposefully intended to treat any one of his followers in a manipulative or autocratic manner. I believe Mitch *was allowed* to be the way he was as he reached the top echelon of his business. How many of his leaders addressed this behavior with him? How many turned a blind eye because he was producing results? This is how this condition is conceived.

How do you avoid entering the toxic track yourself, you might ask? It is important to add that the track is narrow and very few, comparatively, traffic in this track. But your first order of business would be to first evaluate your social skills, specifically how you interact and communicate with others. Do you actively listen and respond with empathy? If you are a conscientious leader, take a look at your willingness to accept the opinion of others and be collaborative in the planning and execution. You will need to relinquish some control and give credit where it is due. In Mitch's situation, he showed little interest in hearing the perspective of others. Because of his experience to find success on his own, he apparently would rather manage solutions in a vacuum. This will guarantee you will enter the toxic track. So be accountable to someone you trust to tell you the truth while being open to their constructive critique. Using a hype man to give you feedback will never lower you on the toxic scale. But a trusted peer or mentor that can identify your behavior's secondary and tertiary effects to the people and the production will bring some enlightenment and a pathway to effective problem solving, improved social skill, and collaborative strategies. I can imagine there are a number of leaders who are unaware of instances with their behavior that comes off as toxic. Because sometimes learned behavior that goes unopposed is condoned. And when it is condoned, it tells you that it is an acceptable behavioral practice. But when you know, it is on you to take ownership of this behavior. Having been touched with the wand of self-awareness, you become solely responsible for it.

Let's be honest, toxic leadership is the hot new buzzword floating around in today's businesses, corporations, military back offices, and anywhere else where a formal organizational structure is designed. There have been plenty of employees that have cried wolf or thrown a penalty flag to make others aware that toxic leadership was being emitted. It has been called out so often that some have even tuned it out. And in some cases, the penalty flag had to be picked up. Let us agree that leaders who are assertive in their communication, speak with candor, or even outwardly show their controlled frustration should not enter the toxic spectrum. But it is those intimidating behaviors that exact fear, humiliate, or discriminate are the ones that clearly rate to the far right on the spectrum's meter. Leaders who also disregard, dismiss, or ignore the conditions or the health of their people should reside within the spectrum. But you should not confuse it with ordering periodic mandatory extra time, choosing an acceptable operational risk, or passing on one for a developmental or promotion opportunity as toxicity. We have to be careful in its use. Toxic leadership is the exercise of severe and persistent disregard and poor behavior that goes beyond hurt feelings. Wrongfully characterizing a leader with this buzzword can be damning and difficult to undo.

So what now?

1. Assume leaders do not aspire to be toxic.
2. Incorporate feedback sessions that open the discussion on personality and toxic leadership.
3. Talk openly about toxic leadership.
4. Deliberately put leaders in positions of power that do not exhibit toxic characteristics.
5. Purposefully delay putting leaders in positions of power when they are not ready.

Spot the one percent who are purposefully

– autocratic	– manipulative
– toxic	– overly competitive
– narcissistic	– discriminatory

[THE NINETEENTH HOLE]

CHAPTER 19

IS IT REALLY?

HAVE YOU EVER NOTICED HOW urban lingo or strange new words that were used in the past take on new meaning? Or notice how new phrases sneak into our vernacular? All of a sudden, you find yourself using those phrases, jargon, or terms and have no earthly idea how you have learned them. Oftentimes people slip in new hip words into the work environment to remain relevant with the new generation of workers. And as much as I agree that you have to find the connection by maybe speaking on their wavelength, leaders have to be careful not to be so hip that they lose their professionalism. I get it—it is hard to come to terms with being out of touch. It is a gut punch initially, but taking the next steps into your leadership journey sometimes means shedding some, not all, of your past activities or behaviors that maybe were a little questionable or borderline unprofessional. Young leaders may even find it overwhelming to balance being cool and relevant and maintaining respect as the leader with marching orders to reach specific goals. Fresh new lingo is often the method some leaders use to remain connected.

This reminds me of a time when I was the command and control operations team leader, tasked to lead an up-tempo deployed operations center and had inherited old, mothballed air-to-ground radios, outdated computers, and single-line analog telephones. Amazingly, this was the same operations center responsible for tracking high-valued detainee transfers, controlling ten to fifteen aircraft arrivals and departures per day, monitoring and detecting adversary missile warnings, and producing daily situation reports to headquarters for this extremely volatile region. The center, logistics node, and communications hub existed to chase down dangerous terrorists, like Abu Musab Al-Zarqawi, Abu Bakr al-Baghdadi, and the late president of Iraq, Saddam Hussein. This was a serious operation. As I took over the responsibility for the operations center, I was debriefed on how the previous team performed operations with this incredibly dilapidated technology. I stood there scanning the operations center, baffled by what I was seeing and hearing. My attention was completely overtaken by a literal rat's nest of communications wiring hanging from the ceiling. I was so disturbed that I did not quite make out what he was saying. It was like I was hearing Charlie Brown's teacher. Out of nowhere, a modicum of clarity: my predecessor said, "Hey, man, it is what it is."

Ugh!

There it is! That global phrase we have somehow embraced—*it is what it is*. It is the phrase that is just subtle enough to say I am not sure, or I don't like it, but I have accepted it. In terms of leadership, *it is what it is* could communicate that you have abdicated your responsibility to take the additional steps to remain accountable to its results. In fact, it could mean that you have accepted defeat. In its most profound usage, *it is what it is* says your situation or position is rendered powerless to influencing alternatives. I am guessing that is not what you mean.

Let's analyze this a little deeper from a leadership perspective. When your employee comes to you as their leader, and you respond with *it is what it is*, you just might leave a sick feeling in their gut as they walk away. They came to you for answers, an explanation, or action. You have a responsibility to fulfill their query. These are the times when you have to step up and take ownership.

Ownership is one of the qualities that middle managers, first-line supervisors, and team leaders look at with ambiguity. I know what you are thinking. How much ownership can I actually take? But leaders have so many ownership alternatives. They have the capacity to take and accept risk, gain perspective, analyze the data and micro-data or, most importantly, they have the ability adapt to situations and solve problems. In leadership, accountability and ownership is the conceded responsibility for actions, products, judgments, and policies. Taking responsibility acknowledges the degree of latitude they hold when it comes to administration and policy, and its implementation. But it is important to include, employees have no leverage to solutions and depend solely on their leaders when situations become uncertain when there is a lack of support, resources, or policy constraints.

Just think if you went to your boss with:

- Ma'am, we didn't screen the luggage because our airport x-ray machines are broken. "It is what it is."
- Sir, we are having a rash of equal opportunity complaints. "It is what it is."

- The torque wrenches used to replace airplane tires are late to being calibrated. "It is what it is."

NATASHA

Natasha was an administrative assistant to a senior officer. She had an amazingly infectious personality. There was not a day that she did not have me cracking up. Natasha was a consummate professional. She served a few years in the military, and her husband was an active-duty sergeant. That made her perfect for the job. Every morning, she made sure everything was situated and everyone understood the direction of the boss. Natasha would even make sure all my visitors would be greeted and put at ease. But there was one thing: she absolutely was not going to do *anything* outside her position description. To her credit, the quality in which she did her work made up for any odd request she would refuse. Early on, I noticed Natasha expressed the popular catch phrase *it is what it is* routinely. Whenever she could not accomplish a task because of some sort of barrier, you would hear her say it. If someone would come to the office with a difficulty requiring her boss's attention, she would say it. If there was a situation that would arise that appeared out of our control, you could bet the first thing she would say, "It is what it is." In fairness to Natasha, I knew what she meant. But the phrase is used so routinely that people who did not know Natasha had to discern what it meant. That was the difficulty with the phrase in this case. Because there was a day when a junior officer was required to report to her boss's office. He began to explain what the issue was to Natasha. She replied, "It is what it is." The junior officer sat waiting for his appointment in bewilderment. I am guessing he was wondering if the boss was even going to help at all. Knowing that response, it did not seem like it. Did Natasha's response mean there was nothing we could do to help? After all, he came for help. Of course, she meant it innocently. But if you are not familiar with the person using the phrase, you lose the context. And in this case, the junior officer was already dismayed prior to seeing the boss. You can wonder if he felt like he was wasting his time. Because if *it is what it is* means there is nothing I can do, even in my position, then that is exactly what it meant.

Natasha and I jokingly talked about the phrase quite a bit over the year that we worked together. Yes, I knew what she meant. But it did not matter if I did. It only mattered to the people she came in contact with as the assistant to the boss. I do not know if Natasha will ever stop using the phrase. But if anything, we understand the genesis of the statement. As lines become part of your vernacular, they become innocuous. But at least for one moment, Natasha will think for one second before using it and put it all in context.

If you think about it, *it is what it is* isn't being communicated at the corporate level. It is a phrase that is being vocalized in lower echelons of the business. There are two reasons. One, at the business level, policy has been dealt by corporate managers, and business-level leaders are reluctant to challenge it. Two, at the corporate level, there is freedom to change whatever is necessary to find success. You can bet that circumstances that leaders are negotiating at the business level are blind spots for the C-suite. And you can best believe they knew they would support a change if it made a difference to the stakeholders, the return on investment, the mission, or shareholder value. As leaders, we are expected to be bold and be creative problem-solvers. We cannot accept this level of ambiguity in our positions. Oftentimes we feel our hands are tied when there is an obvious and an advanced approach to complete a task, but guidance somehow restricts those courses of action. This is what I am absolutely certain about when it comes to policy. Policy is the antithesis of innovation. And innovation comes with risk. Because managers are naturally risk adverse and rather maintain a predictable and steady rate of return or speed of production, challenging business norms will almost always be met with resistance. Having supportive data, rather than anecdotes, will lower their defenses and encourage them to be more open to change. When you present data-driven decisions to the C-suite, you are speaking their language. My point is, instead of *it is what it is*, challenge guidance with risk management, *your* out-of-the-box thinking, or creativity. Examine the data and put a solution on the table. Yes, it may take more than a single encounter to address the issue—it should, especially if it is going to change business rules.

I made this the final chapter to this book because I wanted to leave you with a thought before you put it down and file it away with all of your favorites. The people who know me know I dislike this phrase. It is because I believe leaders should make every effort to resolve the queries of their people. *It is what it is* is the easy way out and requires no effort. I acknowledge there is a point when you are in a pinch, and there is too much stacked against you to achieve resolution. When that is the case, it will be obvious to all who are involved and usually money or the law will be the barriers. But *it is what it is* also prevents you from taking necessary risks. In leadership, challenging the status quo, pushing the envelope, and stamping out "This is how we have always done it" are the bedrocks to risk-taking. If you are not taking risks, you are essentially taking steps backward when compared to your competitors or adversaries. *It is what it is* also closes you off from innovation. Innovation is an essential effort that should be woven into all performance measures. If you are not innovating as a company, you are dying as a company. Successful companies challenge their outcomes, take risks, and innovate. When countering with this line of thinking, it definitely *sounds* like an abdication of accountability. But successful leaders never abandon responsibility while putting their teams in a position to win. *It is what it is* is counterintuitive to an evolutionary mindset. So think deeply before you introduce this or any other hip vernacular to your vocabulary. I am confident you did not intend to respond with, "I chose not to analyze the problem and would rather keep yielding poor results." Oddly, it is synonymous with *it is what it is.*

So, is it really?

AUTHOR'S AFTERWORD

I WROTE THIS BOOK BECAUSE there were leadership confrontations or topics that were ostensibly addressed when it comes to the development of our people. This was my Rev Run exhale after thirty years of experience of leading hundreds and at times thousands of people who were thirsty for leadership development. This book has considerable undertones of emotional intelligence. That was on purpose. In fact, the entire book hints at or explicitly connects with emotional intelligence's five skills: self-awareness, self-control, empathy, motivation, and social skill. I believe leadership is effective when its origin is built from your natural and innate strengths and underpinned by your personal power. Personal power is the vehicle to your leadership characteristics. But when the exercise of leadership stems from legitimate authority or a renewed version of other successful leaders, it comes off as fraudulent. *Extracting the Leader from Within* is a charge to pull from deep inside your personality, character, and values to influence optimal performance in your people and your organization. I would hope you do not shy away from these confrontations as you brave the deep.

The vignettes in each of these chapters are real-life experiences I was a part of or familiar with. I believe experiences are amazing lessons. When you analyze them deeply, there is so much to learn. The vignettes are intended to breathe life into these topical confrontations. Each of these people are people I know. Some of them I know very personally. I am excited to present them to you and mean no harm in describing some negative attributes that were illustrated in the book. I felt if I passed on the more challenging examples, the book would lose its credibility. These are powerful lessons that I would like for you to reflect on and measure yourself against.

There are some leaders who intentionally or unconsciously do not present themselves as an obvious hot talent. In fact, some would admit they are quite ordinary. But when they are extracting the leader from within, their pawn-like strengths are bold and come off as pieces of royalty. Just know that you will feel pressured to be more like the leaders around you, especially the bold and gregarious types. There will be some who will be effective even with a no-nonsense, edgy style. Because of their efficacy, you will feel a need to behave like them. But if you do, you will be constantly trying to copy them, and it will always come off as unnatural and uncomfortable. Even when your personality type is not outward and expressive, you still have so much to offer. Being distracted by the chessboard's stronger appearing pieces will only force you into exile. So do not let introvert, type-A, reasoning, or being Blue on any assessment define you. They are neither positive nor negative. They are only to make you aware of your personal intricacies. These intricacies have strengths of their own. Leaders can be themselves and elevate well beyond their authority by extracting those characteristics that inspire their people from a place of compliance to whole commitment. I wish you luck in your leadership journey.

Enjoy the ride.

Seth

ABOUT THE AUTHOR

DAVID E. SATCHELL was born and raised in Omaha, Nebraska. After enlisting in the United States Air Force in 1990, he earned a bachelor's degree in sociology at the American Military University and a master's degree in human resources at Central Michigan University. During his thirty years of service with the Air Force, Satch navigated the ranks to become Command Chief Master Sergeant of the Air Force. He finished his duty as an advisor to the Secretary of the Air Force, Chief of Staff, and the Chief Master Sergeant of the Air Force. After his retirement in 2020, he transitioned into operations management with Amazon. Satch's leadership style leverages emotional intelligence and situational leadership, and he has developed a reputation for inspiring individuals and teams to increase their performance. He currently resides in Tampa, Florida.